Bead Embroidery Techniques
Volume 4 – Stitches, Design and Construction

by Jamie Cloud Eakin

Published by JCE Publishing
Copyright © 2023 Jamie Cloud Eakin
All rights reserved.
ISBN-979-8853670846

Contents

Intro

This is the final book in the Bead Embroidery Techniques series which began with Volume 1 - Bezels. This was followed by Volume 2 – Edges, and Volume 3 - Attaching/Finishing. Each volume, including this one, is unique and does not repeat details in the previous volumes. Taken together, you will have everything you need to expand your creativity and create your own individual designs. Is this all there is with bead embroidery? Well…. No! There is always more and as new products are introduced, the world of bead embroidery expands to embrace them. So, while this complete series may not be everything there is, it is everything you need for a complete foundation of knowledge for bead embroidery and is everything you need for your creative journey with bead embroidery.

Bead On!

Chapter 1 Designing

One the best aspects of bead embroidery is the ease with which you can create your own unique designs. To do this, it is helpful to have a vocabulary to organize your thoughts and ideas. The following is a system I have used for years. There are basically three types of designs. Of course, there are many variations and combinations.

Single Focal:
The first and most basic is the Single Focal, characterized by one focal point. Variations include a single focal with a drop or with fringe. This design concept includes not only necklaces but also earrings and bracelets.

Examples of Single Focal Designs follow.

Totem Designs:

The second category is the Totem design. These are characterized by more than one focal in the design done in a row. While there are many focals, typically there is one dominant focal. Totems can be created in two different ways. One way is to create the totem on one solid piece of backing. The other is to create in sections and then join the sections together.

The designs that follow were created with a solid backing:

The following Totem designs were created In sections and then joined together:

Collar/Bib Designs

The final category of designs is the Collar or Bib style of design. These are characterized by a larger surface often around the entire neck or at least partway. Like Totem designs, they can be created on one piece of backing or by joining together components that are beaded separately.

Examples of Colar/Bib designs created with a solid backing follow:

These next Collar/Bib designs were created in sections and then joined together:

Now that we have some design definitions and some construction approaches, we'll make some design tools.

Design tools – Necklaces

Neck form page -
A neck form page is simply a circle on a piece of paper that is the size of your neck.

1. Take a piece of string and wrap it around your neck, positioning it where you would want a choker necklace to be placed. Place like it is a strand of pearls, not a dog-collar type of choker. Cut the string so it is exactly the length of your neck.
2. Now arrange the string into a circle with the ends just touching in the center of a piece of paper. Keep the string as round as possible. Use a dark pen and trace where the string is. If you are having trouble creating a circle, get a large canned goods from the kitchen. Trace that circle on the paper and use it to help you place your string.
3. Hold the paper up to a light and fold in half matching the lines as much as possible. Fold in half again (now in quarters) again matching up the lines. Leave folded and cut on the lines to create a circle that represents your neck. Mark the fold lines.
4. Take a new piece of paper and fold in half, then in half again (quarters). Put the circle created in step 3 on the paper and match up the fold lines. Trace around the circle form.

Finally, use a ruler and draw lines on both outside edges. This defines the **key design area**.

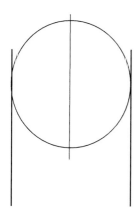

You can create small, medium, and large neck forms. For small, use a string length of 14 Inches, for large, use 18 to 19 inches. See page 105 in the appendix for a neck form page using 14, 15 and 18 inch neck sizes. Keep your neck form page in your workspace and use it to judge proportion and spacings for your design. The key to remember is that this is a flat form but a neck is not flat. When your design approaches and goes beyond the key design area, that portion is up and over the shoulder.

Collar form -
You can easily create a form to use to make a beaded collar using the neck circle above. The collar form includes adjustments to account for the conical shape of the neck and shoulders.

1. Get a piece of paper large enough to accommodate your collar form. Fold in half and mark that as the center line.
2. Use the neck circle from your toolbox (see above). Match up the center lines and trace onto the paper.
3. Draw marks 1/4 inch from the neck circle on the front and sides. Mark 1 inch from the neck back. Draw a line at the 1 inch mark that is 3 ½ inches long (1 ¾ on each side). Connect that line to the other marks, circling the neck. This delineates the inner neck portion for your backing and is larger than the neck circle in the front and on the sides to accommodate edge beading and provide comfort and ease. The shape is not a true circle so that when the back portion is joined, it will create a cone shape to conform with the shape of the body.

Now that you have the inner neck measured, simply draw the area around it to create the beading area of the collar. Shorten the back edge to accommodate the clasp as desired. Fold in half and cut so that each side will match. (see illustrations below).

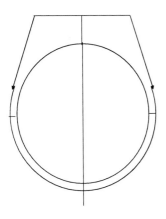 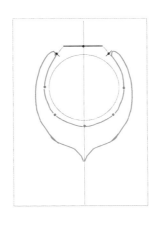 

Tip: Always create a pattern out of paper and try it on before tracing onto the under-backing.

Tip: Create a neck circle and a collar form using cardboard from the back of a tablet. This is sturdy and makes it easy to trace onto paper to use in designing.

See pages 106-108 in the appendix for forms for neck sizes 14, 15 and 18. Remember to adjust the length in the back to accommodate area for the clasp.

The following is an example using a neck form page or a collar form to construct a collar necklace.

Use the collar form to help plan your design.

  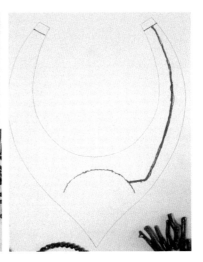

This design will have the round focal attached to the collar with 4mm beads. So, before finalizing the pattern, the focal was beaded first and edged with the Basic edge. Then it was placed on the form with the 4mm beads to determine the cut line and the final pattern was created.

Use your collar form to assist in final construction for placement of components and length of necklace strands.

 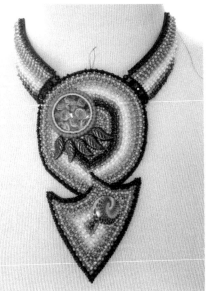 

If you have a full mannequin dress form, use it to test your design during construction.

Design tools – Bracelets

The first thing to recognize is that not all bracelets should fit the same. A wide cuff bracelet is typically worn tighter and higher on the wrist than other styles of bracelets. So, having more than one form on your page is useful.

Bracelet form page -
We will create the bracelet forms page using the same methodology as we used for the neck form page, so go and get some string.

1. Drape the string around your wrist in the area that you want a draped bracelet (like a strand of pearls) to hang. This will typically be approximately one inch down from your wrist but is also a matter of personal preference. Cut the string and measure with a ruler. Draw that length on the bracelet forms page, starting the line at the leftmost side of the page. Label the line "draped". Use a ruler and mark the center with a small vertical line.

2. Take the same string and form into a circle on the page below the line. Draw that circle. Write "draped" inside the circle. Use your judgment and draw a line down the middle of the circle.

3. Use the same string and measure around your wrist again, but this time wrap it up on the wrist where you would wear a watch. Insert one finger under the string increasing the length to add ease for comfort when wearing. Cut the string and measure with a ruler. Draw that length on the bracelet forms page centered below the circle in 2 above. Label the line "cuff". Use a ruler and mark the center with a small vertical line.

4. Finally, set your wrist down on the paper, centered and below the line drawn in 3 above. Draw a short line on each side that will mark the width of your wrist. Lift your wrist up and connect the two lines with a ruler. Label the line "width". This designates a key design area.

Keep this handy by your bead station to assist with designing.

Another type of bracelet form can be made from a strip of paper. Cut a strip using your favorite width. Wrap it around your wrist and cut to fit as desired. Mark the center. You can also mark the ends to account for the clasp.

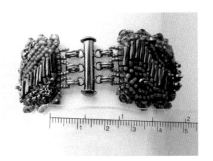

Tip: Use a previous creation to calculate how much length is needed for the clasp.

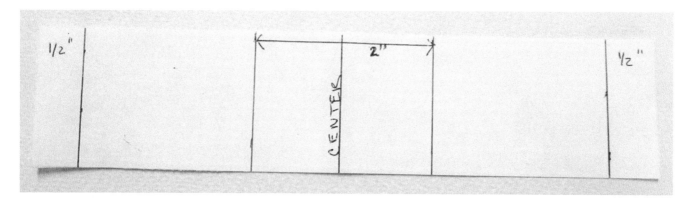

Mark the center. Mark area for the clasp as desired. Mark 2 inches in the middle to designate the key design area.

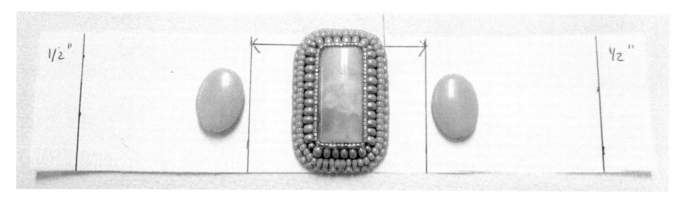

Use the form to lay out your design and to measure against during construction.

Cuffs -

Cuff bracelets have a unique attribute that Single focal bracelets do not have; cuff designs bend throughout the beaded area of the bracelet. This bending can open up spaces between the beads and expose the under-backing.

There are three ways to address this.

1. One is to select a backing with an acceptable appearance so that when it shows, it looks fine. Ultra Suede and Cork fabrics work well for this
2. Another method is to design around the issue. The exposure is most severe when there are rows of beads that parallel the bended area. Stitching rows on angles in those areas will solve this problem.

3. Finally, you can stitch beads over the exposure areas. Bezel rows automatically do that since it is a row in between the focal and the base row surrounding it. Create stacks, or stitch another row on top and midway between other rows to hide exposed areas.

Hard cuffs: (see Vol 3 Attaching/Finishing)

1. Get your hard cuff form.
2. Create a pattern on paper based on the cuff surface that is at least ¼ inch larger on all sides. Cut out the pattern; test it on the cuff form. Adjust as necessary.
3. Use the pattern to draw on the under-backing. Trim and bead the backing as desired.
4. Apply glue to the outside of the cuff form and apply the beadwork. Make sure you have edges beyond the cuff form on all sides. The easiest way to do this is to start at one end, and wrap to the other end

5. Now use the pattern again. Draw on the outer backing and cut on the lines.
6. Apply glue to the inside of the cuff form. Start at one end and apply the outer backing matching the end and sides. Wrap around the inside to the other end. You will need to trim the last end to match the beaded backing size. Although these were created with the same pattern, one is outside the cuff and the other is inside, so they end up to be different lengths because of the curve.

Final note:
Other examples showing the use of these design tools are included in the remainder of the book.

Chapter 2 Construction

The steps used for bead embroidery are generally the same for any project.
1. Plan your design.
2. Select and prepare your backing.
3. Sew the beads on according to your design.
4. Review your beaded piece. Usually there is a spot or two (or many more!) that need one more bead sewn in. Fill in as needed.
5. Trim (if not already trimmed).
6. Select the outer-backing and glue on, after inserting a stabilizer (see page 26) if desired.
7. Trim the outer-backing.
8. Bead the edges, which will sew the beading under-backing to the outer-backing.
9. Finish by adding edge embellishments, and/or attaching other beaded strands and findings.

There are many ways for the creative process to happen. Generally, you will have an idea of the type of project you want to do like a necklace, purse, earrings, pillow cover, etc. Start by assembling the key components and have some "play time" arranging them and imagining the final design using the concepts of single focal, totem and collar/bib. Use your design tools from the previous chapter to assist developing ideas and provide scale and proportion. Make a rough sketch or use your cell phone to take a picture of your layout. Taking a photo is also helpful as you develop your plan: take a picture, then move the beads into another design and take a new picture, repeat. Then select the picture you like best.

Once you have the preliminary design decided, assemble all the other beads and components for your project. Create a pattern from paper of your design and

mark it as needed. Be sure to try on your pattern! Now prepare your backing. Make sure the backing is sufficient to hold the weight of the beads and components selected. Use your pattern and trace the outline on the backing. If you are using a non-fray backing (e. g. Lacys Stiff Stuff, starched felt, cork fabric), you can cut on the outline now or wait until the beading is done. If your design is a specific shape, I recommend cutting out the shape at the beginning. It is usually easier to sew the beads near the edge than risking cutting threads when the shape is cut after beading. If you are using a backing that frays and you want to cut out the pattern now, use a no-fray glue or treatment to the edges of the backing.

There are 4 basic methods for constructing bead embroidery. Each has advantages, and is often just a personal preference of the individual beader.

Method 1 – Start with gluing on all the components

Once you have your plan, glue all the major components on, then bead. This is a totem design with a Plain/Standard Bezel. The plan is for the components to share the base row beads, so I used a length of those beads to determine the spacing between the components before gluing the component to the backing.

For the next example, I used the collar form tool and placed the components down to plan a shape to use. The pattern was made and tested, then the backing cut. The components were glued down, then each was stitched on.

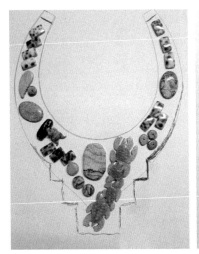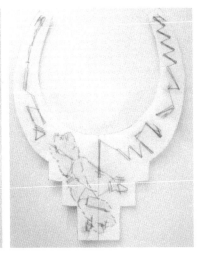

The remaining areas were filled with beads, then backing, edging and finishing.

Method 2 – Glue on components as you bead

Plan the bead placement. Select the largest and/or most strategically important ones first, and glue on and stitch the bezel and other beads. Continue adding to create your design like a building process. This method allows you to adjust the spacing and design as needed. If your plan is for a row or rows of beads between two components, sew on those rows (or the key part of the row) before gluing the second bead/component to get the placement just right.

In the example photos that follow, the collar form was used to plan and then create a pattern from paper. Key lines were drawn on the backing to assist with bead placement later. The first component was glued on and bezeled. Other components were glued on, stitched on and bezeled where necessary.

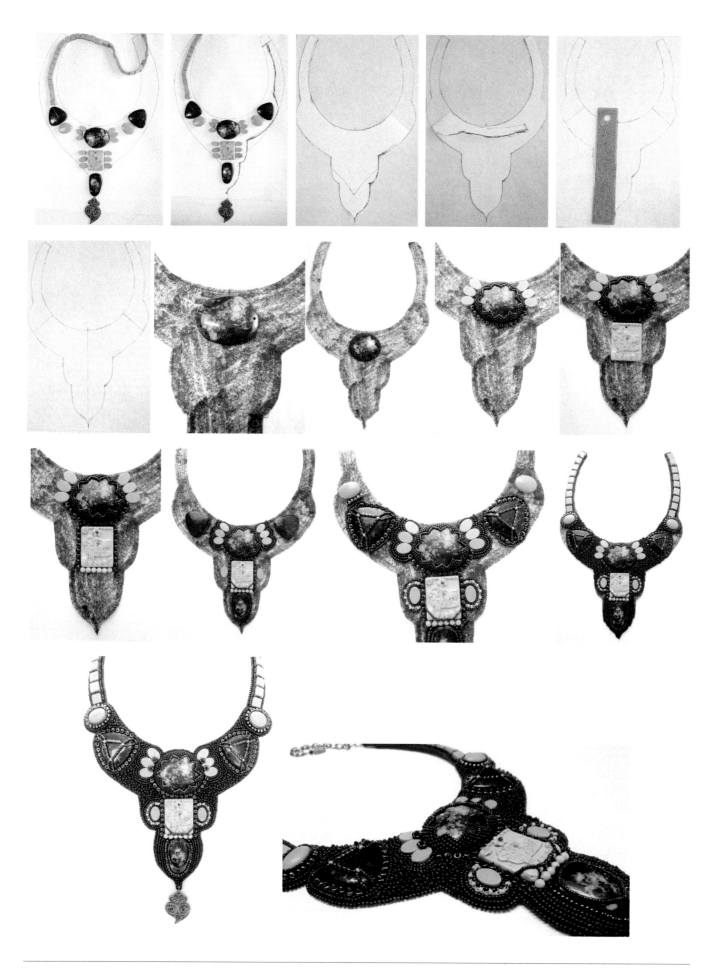

Method 3 – Bead the components then add
This method is a hybrid of the first two methods
where you bead components separately and then
add to a full backing. You can re-arrange the design
as you bead. Bead the components and trim as
close as possible then stitch the beaded
components to the full backing using a Sewing
Backstitch (page 65).

Method 4 – Pieced

Pieced designs are fun and easy to create. Bead each component then combine into the finished design. The advantage to this approach is that it is easy to dramatically change your design up until the very end. Once the components are beaded, have some play time with different arrangements before finalizing your design.

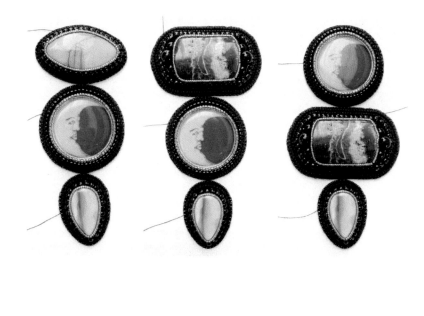

In the pictures that follow, the collar form was used to plan the design. Next, the components were created and the collar form was used to finalize the plan. Trace around the placement and label. Use a sticky label to mark the components. Stitch the components together, starting in the middle top.

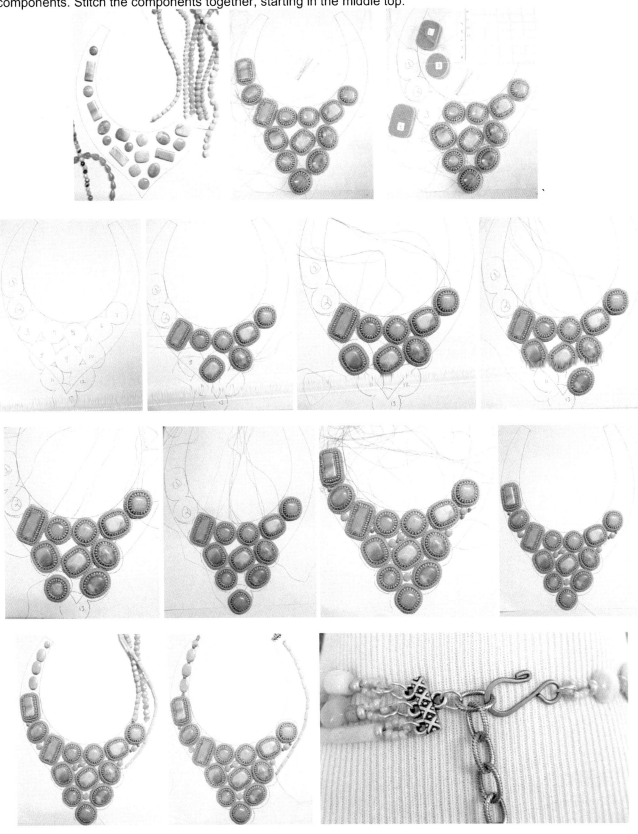

Leftover components are great to use to make other designs or save for the future.

Tip: Do a partial trim
When creating a collar, glue on the outer backing and trim the outside edges only. Bead the outside edges. Finally, trim the inside of the collar and finish the edge beading. Waiting to trim the inside collar edge gives a stability to the piece as you bead the outside edges.

Enlarging under-backing –

Under-backing can be easily extended. This can be done in the planning stage to make the under-backing larger to fit large designs. Sometimes, as in the example below, the plan changes as you are beading and you need to extend the backing to accommodate a design change (photo 1).

Steps –
1. Cut a new piece of backing and line up with the previous piece (photo 2)
2. Stitch the pieces together using a slip stitch across the row. Repeat back across the row (photo 3).
3. Continue with your design (photos 4-6).

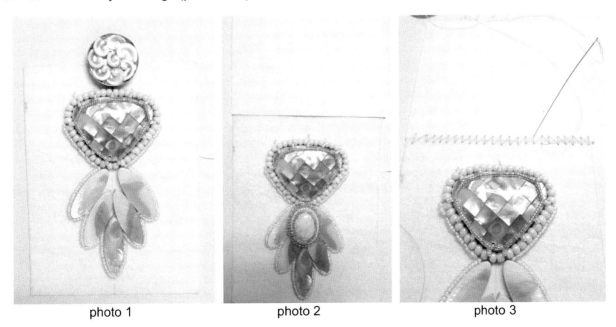

| photo 1 | photo 2 | photo 3 |

photo 4   photo 5   photo 6

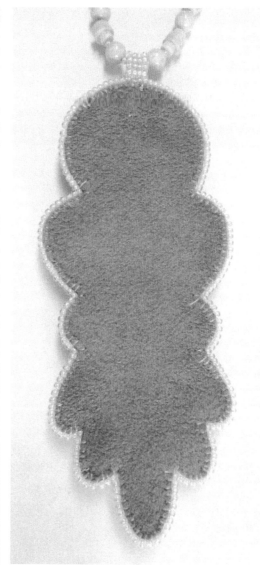

Preparing and Marking backings

It is often helpful to have guidelines on the backing when creating a design. These can help with placement of components or stitches. For more complicated designs, you may choose a gridline. Mark the backing using a permanent marker before gluing any components. In the design below, a dark blue backing was selected so the gridlines would be easy to see. You can mark on a black backing using a white gel pen or dressmaker's pencil but in this case the blue was easier. After all beading that required the marking was done, a black permanent marker was used to color the backing.

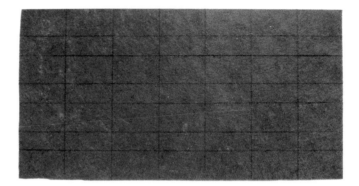

Sometimes a simple marking of the center top and sides of a focal is all that is needed. Place the focal on a piece of paper and trace around it with a dark pen. Hold the paper up to a strong light and fold in half matching the outlines through the paper. Repeat folding in quarters. Mark the fold lines with pen. Now cut out the focal area and place on the backing. Trace around the paper and use a ruler to extend the center lines. Finally, glue the focal to the backing in the marked area. In the example below, the focal is transparent and if lines were marked in the area of the focal, the lines would show so using this process was perfect.

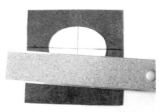

A focal can be centered without marking lines on the backing. Trace around the focal on a piece of paper. Fold in half (hold up to the light and match the outlines). Cut out the tracing. Use the pattern folded in half and match up to the backing. Place the tracing between the backing and pattern while matching up the center lines. Remove the pattern and mark the backing around the tracing.

  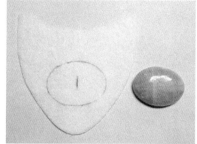 

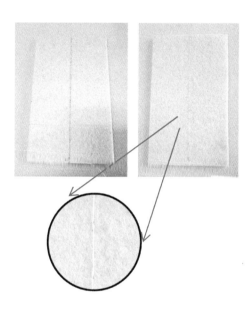

There are cases where there is a concern about markings on the backing showing in the final design. This is often true with white beads on white backing, and black beads on black backing. For those designs, mark the underside of the backing. Then use a matching thread and stitch a line of thread on the marked areas. These lines will be visible as you bead but will not show through the beadwork. Use a backstitch or running stitch (page 65) to create the stitches.

Stabilizers

There are times when a project requires more stiffness, or stability than is provided by the backings. You can add stiffness by inserting a stabilizer between the backing and outer-backing (in red figure 1). If you simply want to add smoothness to the backing to cover for a lumpy beaded backing, thin plastic is recommended. Office supply stores carry plastic report covers that work well for this purpose. For a stiffer stronger stabilizer, flashing is recommended. Flashing is a metal used in construction/roofing and is available at hardware stores. It is thin, but stiff and can easily be cut with tin snips, or a pair of heavy, strong scissors. Plastic from an empty milk or juice carton is also useful, readily available, and easy to cut.

First, create a "pattern" using paper. Lay the trimmed embroidery piece down and trace the outside edge. Cut the paper approximately ¼ inch in from the traced edge to create a pattern. Lay the pattern on the flashing or plastic, trace and cut. Measure against the actual beaded piece and trim if needed. Be careful to leave space around the edge and any other area where more stitching will be done. Glue the flashing to the backing. When the glue is dry, apply the outer-backing as usual. It usually is not necessary to cover the entire back of the piece especially with large jewelry pieces since some flexibility is often preferable to accommodate body curves.

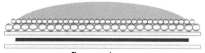

figure 1

Chapter 3 Stitches

Bead embroidery stitches apply beads to the surface of a backing. The backing can be totally covered or simply have beads in strategic places to create a design. When you are starting out with a project, you may struggle with stitch/bead placement, trying to be precise with the stitching. However, you will find that as the beads fill the surface, the placement of any individual bead is affected by the beads that surround it. Rows become smoother because of the surrounding rows. Beads get "nudged" into place by the beads next to them. So, relax and enjoy the synergies of bead embroidery.

1. Use single thread, except where indicated.
2. Pull the thread firmly so the beads are secure; however, do not pull so tightly that you bend, twist, or torque the backing. In other words, keep the surface of the backing flat.

Adding/Ending thread.

Use a thread length that is easy to work with. While two yards is good as a general rule, it can differ from one beader to another. Adding a thread and ending a thread is the same process in bead embroidery. Stitch the thread back and forth into the backing using at least three-quarters inch for the stitch length and a count of three stitches. Be careful to do this in an area of the backing that is covered by beads so the thread doesn't show on the front of the work (it will be underneath the beads). This will result in a flat surface without a lump from a knot. Even though the back will be covered with an outer-backing, having a smooth surface will improve the appearance.

When beginning a project, it may be difficult to identify where to stitch. In that case, simply leave a 9 inch tail thread to weave in later when you can identify where to weave the thread end. If desired, add a Half-Hitch knot before the weave to better hold the thread tension (or after the weave when adding thread). This is a small knot so it has very little impact on the final appearance of the backside.

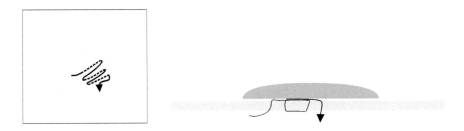

One bead stitch

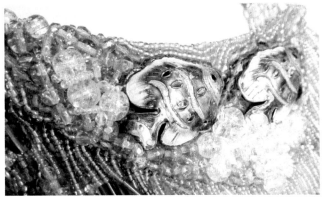

Simply stitching one bead can create fabulous designs. If a bead is large, it is often easiest to glue it down before stitching. Glue dots used for scrapbooking come in various sizes as small as 5mm and are permanent and acid free. Double stick tape also comes acid free and can be cut to any size. When using the glue dots, be sure to keep the needle away from it or it will gum up your needle and thread.

Steps-
1. Determine the position you want the bead to be with the bead hole parallel to the backing.
2. Stitch up to the topside directly under one of the bead holes.
3. Stitch through the bead and down the backing directly under the other side of the bead hole.
4. Repeat steps 2 and 3. For beads larger than 4mm or size 5 seed, repeat again.

If the bead is large (more than 8mm) and is curved, stitch through the backings next to the area where the bead touches the surface instead of directly under the bead holes (figure 2). This will allow the thread to be pulled tightly without altering the flatness of the backing. Stitch through the bead at least three times, spreading the stitches as shown in figure 3 instead of all stitches lined up with the bead hole.

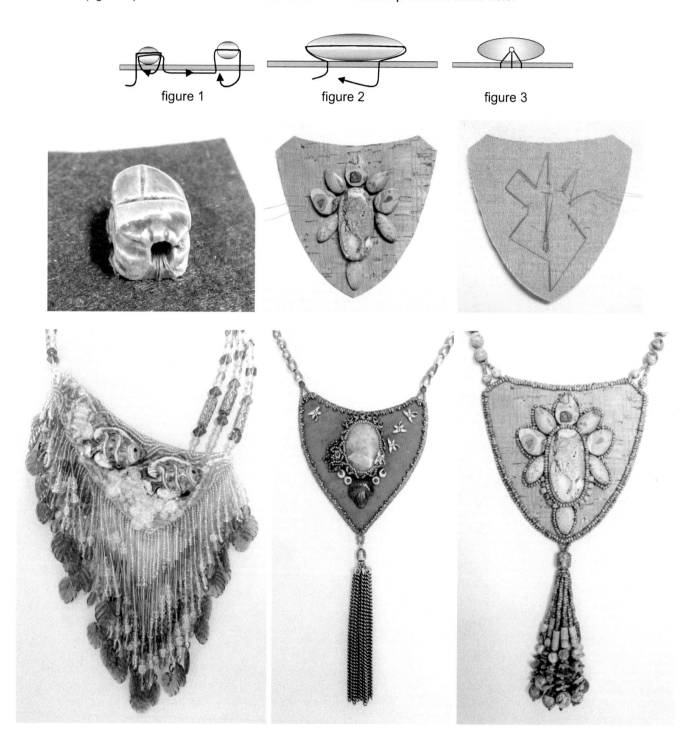

figure 1   figure 2   figure 3

Backstitch

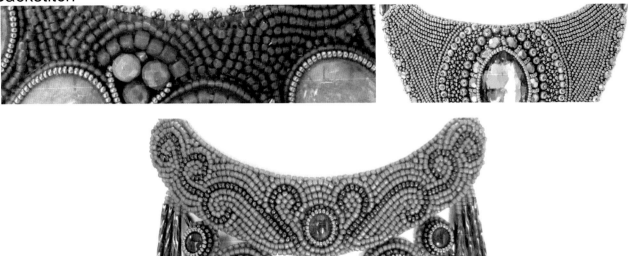

Backstitch is the most widely used stitches in bead embroidery. It is used to create a row of beads. Use it to create a pattern, provide texture, or to paint a picture. Typically, it is done with size 11 seed beads, but it is also a great stitch to use with smaller or larger seed beads and other kinds of beads as long as the desired result is a row of beads.

There are many variations of the Backstitch. For example, 1-1 Backstitch, 2-3 Backstitch, 4-2 Backstitch,

and 4-6 Backstitch are all common variations. Each can be used whenever a Backstitch process is called for and is often a choice of what the individual beader feels most comfortable using and is more proficient at. The first number identifies how many beads to pick up and add to the row while the second number identifies how many beads to count backwards in the row to stitch back up to the top and though. All of the variations use the same steps, only the counts for the beads changes.

Tip: The 4-6 Backstitch covers areas faster, and with a smoother line than many other variations. However, when beading a tight curve or corner, switch to a 2-3 Backstitch. You can switch the bead count (and back again) within a beaded row as desired.

Steps for Backstitch

1. Pick up the count of beads in the first number and stitch down into the backing in a forward direction.
2. From the under-side, count backwards (including the added beads) and stitch up to the top-side. When counting backwards, use the count of the second number.
3. Finally, stitch through the holes of the beads again. The number of beads being stitched through will equal the second number.
4. Repeat until the row is complete.

2-3 Backstitch: Pick up 2 beads and stitch down. Count backwards 3 and stitch up. Stitch through the 3 beads.

4-2 Backstitch: Pick up 4 beads and stitch down. Count backwards 2 and stitch up. Stitch through the 2 beads.

4-6 Backstitch: Pick up 4 beads and stitch down. Count backwards 6 and stitch up. Stitch through the 6 beads

Starting the row –

When starting a row of 4-6 Backstitch (or any variation where the second number counted backwards is greater than the first number of beads added), there are not enough beads on the backwards count. In those cases, stitch up from the backing leaving room to add the additional number of beads needed for the backwards count. Pick up those additional beads, and then stitch through the row.

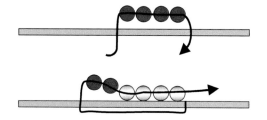

Tip: The stitch through the beads with needle and thread creates friction and pulls the beads forward and create spaces between the beads in the row. Use your fingers and push the beads back into position before stitching through the backing. Continue to push the beads backwards in the row as you bead for a tight, smooth row.

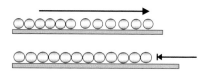

Tip: When stitching multiple rows of Backstitch whether a straight line or curves, it is usually easier to stitch in one direction than the other. Once a row is completed, stitch up to the topside and through the bead holes to travel back to the starting spot. Be careful not to pull the thread too tightly and pull the beads out of place. Stitch down into the backside, then up positioning the needle to create the next row. This process will also straighten the beads.

Tip: If you are stitching a row of Backstitch that is not surrounded by any other beads, consider stitching through the holes multiple times. This will fill up the holes in the beads with the thread and line up the beads more smoothly.

This is a great stitch to use to fill areas while creating a design.

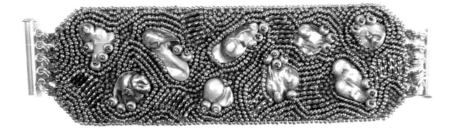

Couch stitch

The Couch Stitch creates a row of beads just like Backstitch and can be used any time a row of beads is desired. This stitch allows the designer to "fit" an entire row of beads from one point to another. Seed beads (even large ones like size 2) have variations in their length so culling (selecting certain beads) will allow for fitting as you create the row. However, other beads (even small ones like a 3mm round) have a consistent size so using them to fit into a defined length or area is more difficult. Using the Couch Stitch for these types of

beads is recommended for rows of a specific length. Because the beads for the entire row are selected at the beginning, you can adjust and fit the beads into a space more effectively than you can when using Backstitch. You can see immediately if the fit is possible and be able to make adjustments. The Couch Stitch is recommended when creating a row of beads around a focal when using consistently sized beads like a 4 or 6mm round.

Steps for Couch Stitch
1. Pick up the desired number of beads and stitch down into the backing in a forward direction creating the bead row (figure 1).
2. Anchor the beads (couch) by stitching up through the backing at the intersection of the nearest two beads. Loop over the thread between the beads and stitch back down into the backing. Pull until the loop over is just above the thread line and hidden between the beads (figure 2). Do not pull so tightly that the thread from step 1 is pulled down toward the backing

Repeat the anchoring/couching process in Step 2 from the end of the row, back to the beginning. For larger beads (4mm or larger), couch the beads (the loop/anchor) between each bead. For seed beads, couch every bead, every two beads or every three beads as desired.

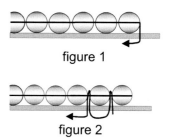

figure 1

figure 2

Tip: If you are stitching a long length of couch stitch or stitching a curve(s), it is easier if there are anchors at several key places as needed to hold the shape of the row before stitching between each bead.

Steps for Couch Stitch around a focal

1. Stitch up the backing near the focal edge. Pick up beads in a quantity to fit around the focal. (photo 1) Test the fit and add or removed beads as needed. (photo 2) If the choice is only between too many beads (so that the row bows out and does not lie next to the focal edge) or too few beads (there are gaps where the thread shows), then select the option of too few beads. Spread/space the beads evenly around the focal so the gaps (if any) are small. (Note: if the gaps are simply too large, consider changing to a different bead or changing the design adding in another size bead. Even beads labeled with a certain size can be slightly larger or smaller

since the size designation is often not a true, calibrated size.)

2. Once the number of beads needed to fit is decided, stitch through the row again (photos 3 and 4). Repeat as desired to add strength and stability to the row. Stitch down into the backing. (photo 5).

3. Space the beads around the focal. Do a couch stitch at 12, 3, 6, and 9 (like on a clock) to anchor and hold the spacing. Respace after each stitch if needed.

4. Do a couch stitch between each bead. End on the backside

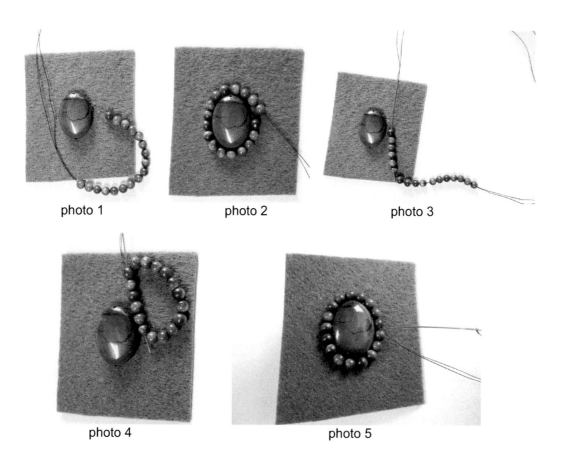

photo 1   photo 2   photo 3

photo 4   photo 5

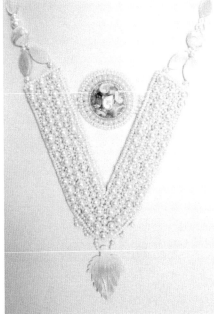

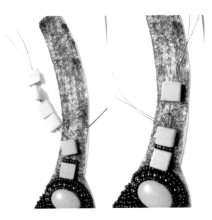

Another way to use the couch stitch is the 2-needle method. Use one needle (typically with doubled thread) to create the row. Use a second needle (typically single thread) to couch. You can create and stitch down with the first needle or, as in the photos below, move the beads down the row one at a time and stitch.

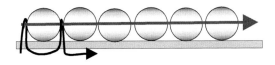

Variations-
Now let's explore some surface designs that combine the One Bead stitch and Couch stitch.

Dots/bubbles
This technique is a wonderful surface design that uses a 4mm round and size 11 seed beads.

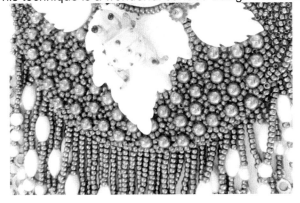

Steps –

1. Stitch on a 4mm bead using the One Bead stitch. (figure 1)
2. Stitch a row around the 4mm bead. Since the fit of the beads is important, use the Couch stitch for this row. Pick up size 11 seed beads and test the fit around the 4mm bead. When judging the fit, too small is better than too long. Couch the row down every 2 or 3 beads. (figure 2)
3. Repeat from step 1. (figures 3-9)
4. Finalize by reviewing the area covered. Use the One Bead stitch with size 11 or 15 seed beads to fill holes as needed.

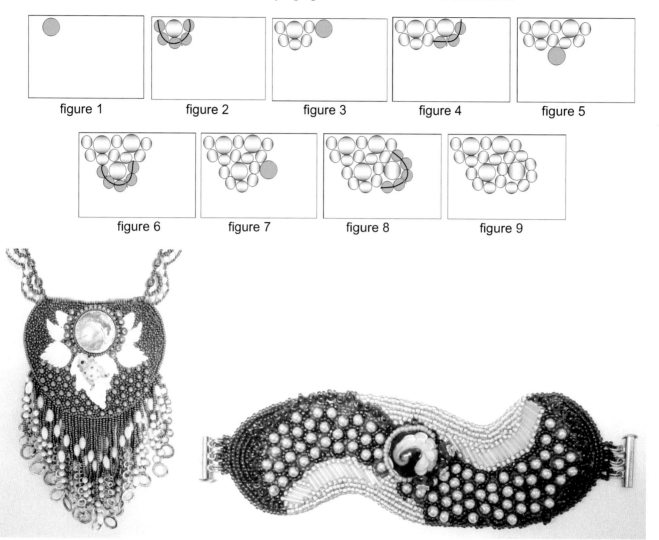

figure 1   figure 2   figure 3   figure 4   figure 5

figure 6   figure 7   figure 8   figure 9

Scallops

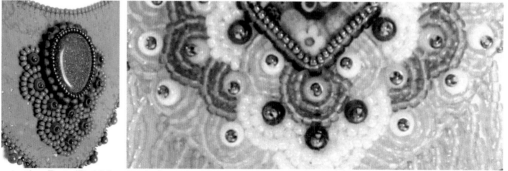

This is similar to the Dots/Bubbles technique but has more rows of seed beads.

Steps –
1. Stitch on a bead using the One Bead stitch. (figure 1) A good choice is a 4mm round, or select a size 6 seed bead using the Stacks stitch.
2. Stitch a row around the 4mm bead. Since the fit of the beads is important, use the Couch stitch for this row. Pick up size 11 seed beads and test the fit around the 4mm bead. When judging the fit, too small is better than too long. Couch the row down every 2 or 3 beads. (figure 2)
3. Stitch an additional row of seed beads using the Couch stitch like step 2. (figure 3)
4. Repeat step 3 for the desired number of rows, typically 2 to 5 total rows.
5. Repeat from step 1. (figures 4-10)

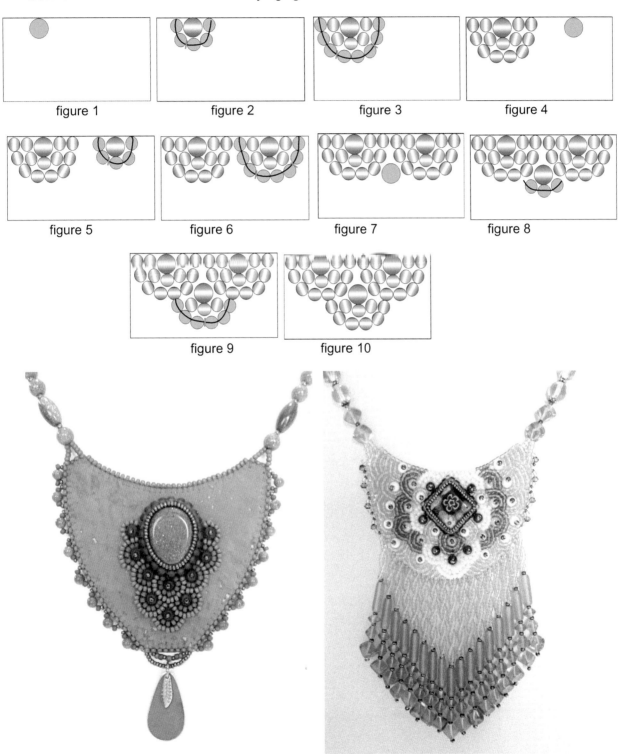

figure 1   figure 2   figure 3   figure 4

figure 5   figure 6   figure 7   figure 8

figure 9   figure 10

Stack Stitch

When you stitch using the One Bead Stitch, the hole is parallel to the surface but with the Stacks Stitch, the hole is perpendicular to the surface. Turning the bead this way provides a very different appearance and texture. You can easily add texture and change the height of the surface with the Stacks Stitch. The stitch is performed just like regular fringe that hangs from an edge but is stitched onto a backing area. Like fringe, there is a bead (or beads) and a turn-bead. You can create fun and interesting designs simply using the Stack stitch and various shapes of beads

Steps -
1. Pick up the stack bead(s) shown in grey in figure 1 plus a turn-bead (red in figure 1).
2. Move all the beads down to the surface of the backing. Skip the turn bead and stitch back through the stack bead(s) and through the backing to the under-side. Hold and pull the turn-bead with one hand while pulling the thread with the other hand to adjust the tension.
3. Stitch up to the top-side in the next placement area and repeat.

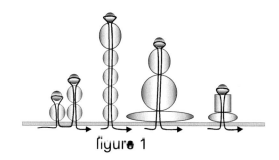

figure 1

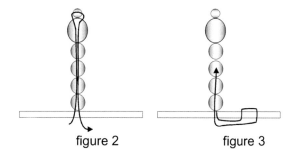

figure 2   figure 3

Stacks may be stitched with many beads and many types of beads increasing their weight. Tall stacks can be stressed or pulled if the item (eyeglass case or purse) experiences rough handling from being rubbed or tossed around. The stress or weight can be addressed by using doubled thread, or stitching through the stack again. Be sure to provide an adequate base area between the stack stitches to provide that strength. (figures 2 and 3)

If stacks are close together skip two or more stacks over to create the stacks so that the area of the backing between5stitches is wider and stronger. Fill in the skipped areas later. Figure 4 shows the recommended approach. In figure 3 (not recommended), there is very little material between the stack stitches so if a stack is pulled strongly, that small area could tear

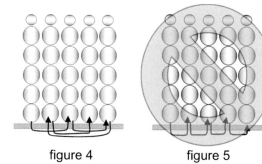

figure 4   figure 5

The Stack stitch can be used in many ways.

These Stacks were stitched in rows.   These Stacks provide texture and add accents.

And, yes, Stacks can also be used as an area fill.

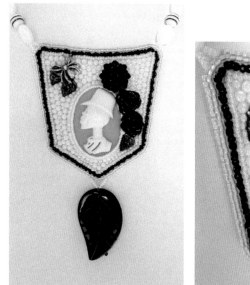

For added height, use bugles in your stacks.

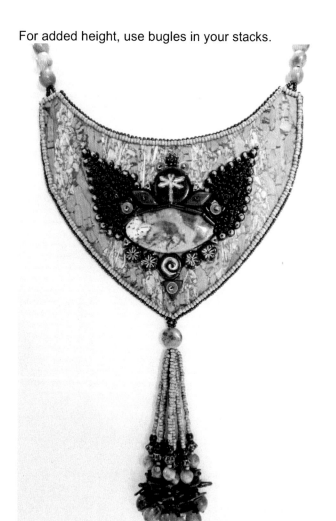

In the example below the Stacks stitch was used with a large bead for the base. The bottom bead was stitched on to provide stability, then the stack was added on top showing the versatility of this stitch to hide or enhance.

Picot/Moss

 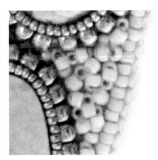

This stitch creates a fabulous texture like a nubby carpet of beads. Use it to fill in an area on the backing where you desire some bulk and/or texture. This stitch is easy to use as a fill-in for areas both large and small. It is especially useful when the area to cover is an irregular shape and small. Any size of beads can be used and you can mix the bead sizes even within the stitch. Beads larger than size 8 seed beads will need double thread to accommodate the added weight. Colors can be monochromatic or as varied as you want.

Steps -
1. Stitch up to the topside from the backside two bead widths from the end.
2. Pick up three beads.
3. Stitch down one bead width backwards. Pull until the middle bead rests on top of the other two beads. (figure 1)
4. Repeat steps 1 through 3 as desired. (figures 2, 3)
The first and third beads are the base beads and the center bead is the topper.

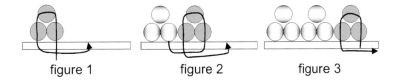

figure 1   figure 2   figure 3

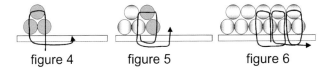

figure 4   figure 5   figure 6

Fuller variation
You can create a row that is denser by adding more topper beads. Begin the same way, but when adding the next set, pick up only two beads and stitch down into the previous base bead.

For a more random appearance, outline the area to be covered alternating the direction of the picot as illustrated below. Repeat around the entire border of the area to be covered. Then, fill in the center with picots, changing directions; horizontal, vertical and on a slant.

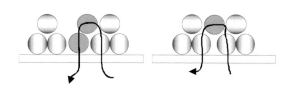

When filling in, if there is an area that only one bead will fit, stitch up to the top through one of the base beads of one of the previous picots. Pick up two beads and stitch down into the area to fill. If there is an area to fill in that will not accommodate any base beads, stitch up through the base bead of a previous picot, pick up one bead and stitch down through the base bead of another previous picot.

Add a row of Picot/Moss stitch for a different texture

Fill an area – the area can be large or very small

Do rows of Picot/Moss stitch to fill an area and change the bead colors.

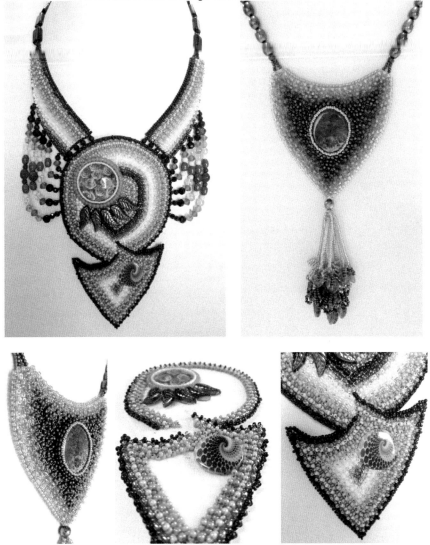

Circles

This technique adds wonderful texture. It is like the Circles Edge (Vol 2) but is stitched on the surface.

Steps –

1. Start with a row of Picot/Moss stitch with the Fuller Variation and using a size 15 bead as the topper. (page 39)
2. Stitch up the base bead and through the topper bead. Pick up 7 size 15 beads. (figure 1)

3. Stitch back through the topper bead entering on the other side of the bead than the one the thread is exiting to create a circle and stitch down through the base bead below. (figure 2)
4. Repeat from step 2 using the next base bead. (figures 3,4)

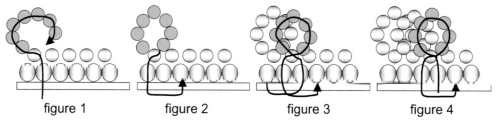

figure 1   figure 2   figure 3   figure 4

Multi row Circles stitch

When stitching multiple rows of Circles stitch, add a row of Backstitch in between the rows of Circle stitch. Add all the rows, then complete the circles stitching the innermost row first and working outwards.

Raised bead row

Use this technique when you want to give more height to a row.

Steps –

1. Start with a row of Picot/Moss stitch (page 39). You can use size 11 or size 15 for the topper bead as desired for the top row of beads.
2. Switch to doubled thread for the next steps.
3. Stitch up through the last base bead and through the topper. Pick up beads as needed to span the distance to the next topper bead.

4. Repeat step 3 across the row. End stitching down in the base bead. If desired stitch up again through a base bead and through the row again to make it smoother.

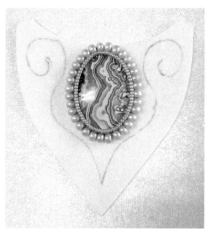  

Twist Stitch

This is a fun stitch to add texture and height to the surface. This is like the Twisted Edge stitch (Vol 2) but done on the surface.

Steps –

1. Start with a row of Picot/Moss stitch (page 39) using size 11 seed beads for the topper. Use the color selected for the twist. For a two-color twist, alternate the topper bead color.
2. Stitch up the last base bead.
3. Stitch through the topper. Pick up beads to span the distance to the topper bead two

topper beads away plus one or two beads to create a loop.
4. Repeat step 3 across the row. End down through the base bead.
5. Repeat from step 2 coming up the base bead near the topper not used. Twist the added beads around the previous loops.

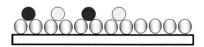 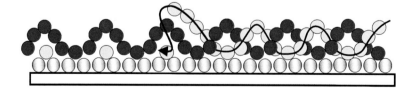

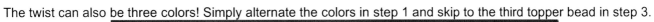

The twist can also be three colors! Simply alternate the colors in step 1 and skip to the third topper bead in step 3.

Loop Stitch

This stitch is just like the Picot/Moss stitch except there are more than three beads. Use the instructions for the Picot/Moss stitch (page 39) except pick up as many beads as desired instead of just three. In the following example, The Loop stitch was used in graduating heights with various colors.

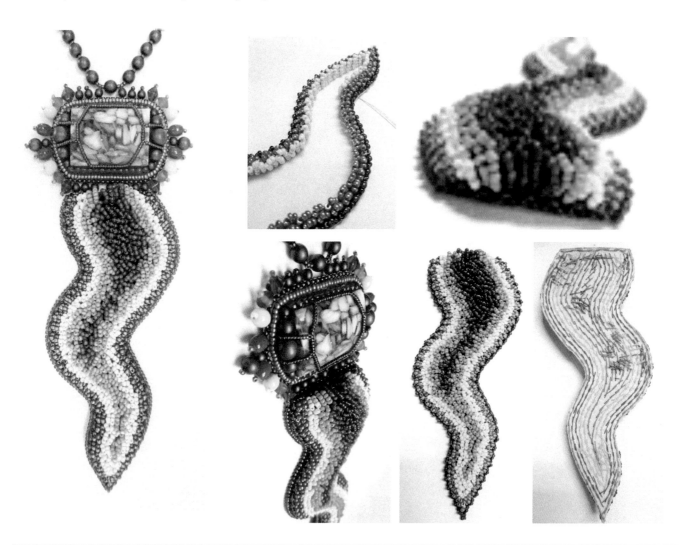

In this example, the top focal that was bezeled with the Loop-stack bezel (Vol 1). Next was a row of Loop stitch with 11 beads followed by a row of 4mm beads and then a row of Loop Stitch with 5 beads. It was finished with a row of Backstitch using size 15 beads. The combination works to blend the tall focal into a slope to the edge

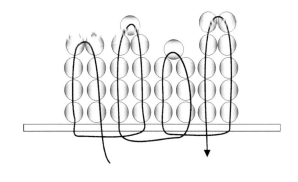

The next design Includes the Loop stitch in used various heights for an interesting fill.

Lazy Stitch
This stitch covers an area with beads quickly and can create interesting textures.

Steps-
Use doubled thread for rows longer than 5 beads or for bead sizes larger than a size 11 seed beads.

1. Stitch up from the backside at the top of the row.
2. Pick up the desired number of beads.
3. Stitch down into the backing leaving space for the beads, at the bottom of the row.
4. To add the next row, stitch up to the topside again at the top of the row.
5. Repeat steps 2 through 4 as desired.

In the examples that follow, the Lazy stitch is used with bugle beads. When using bugle beads, examine them closely since many bugle beads have sharp edges. If that is the case, use a seed bead, then bugle, then seed bead for the row so the bugle beads do not cut the thread.

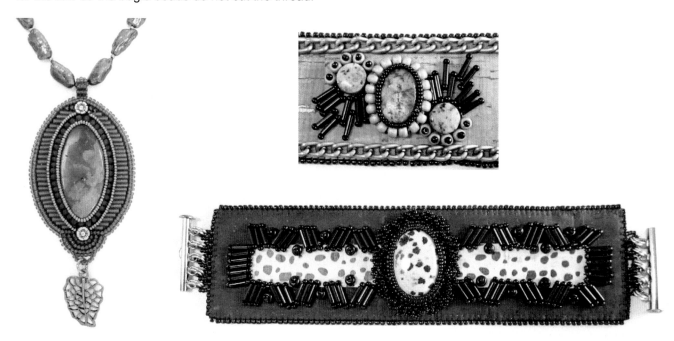

Cross Hatch Lazy Stitch

This variation is a wonderful way to fill an area. Start with a five-bead stitch and do four rows. Change direction and repeat. Continue until the inside area is covered adjusting the row and bead count as needed.

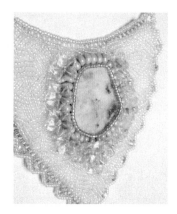

Lazy Ladder Stitch

This stitch combines the Lazy stitch with the Ladder stitch. It is useful when the number of beads in the row is long and is wonderful when you want to use a loom pattern in bead embroidery.

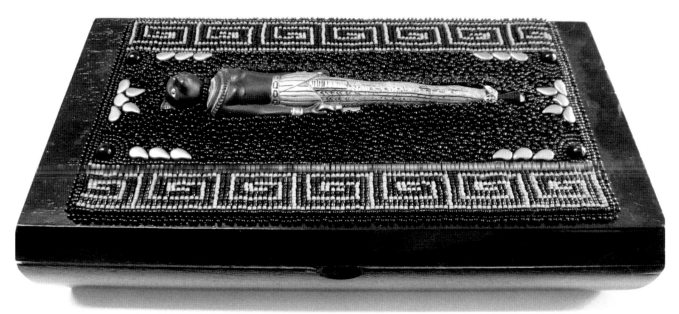

Steps-
1. On a long needle, pick up beads for a whole row. Mark on the backing a line for the top and the bottom using the length of the beads. Remove the beads and mark the backing.
2. Stitch up from the backing at the top. Pick up beads for the row and stitch down through the backing for the row. (figure 1)
3. Stitch up from the backing at the top of the row. (figure 2)
4. Stitch through the row beads. Pick up beads for the next row and stitch through the previous row again. (figure 3).
5. Stitch down through the backing at the bottom of the previous row, then up through the backing at the top of the new row. (figure 4)
6. Repeat from step 4. (figures 5-8)

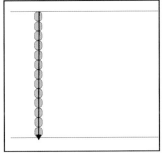

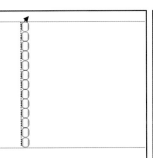

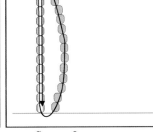

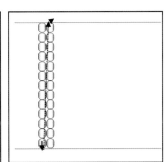

| figure 1 | figure 2 | figure 3 | figure 4 |

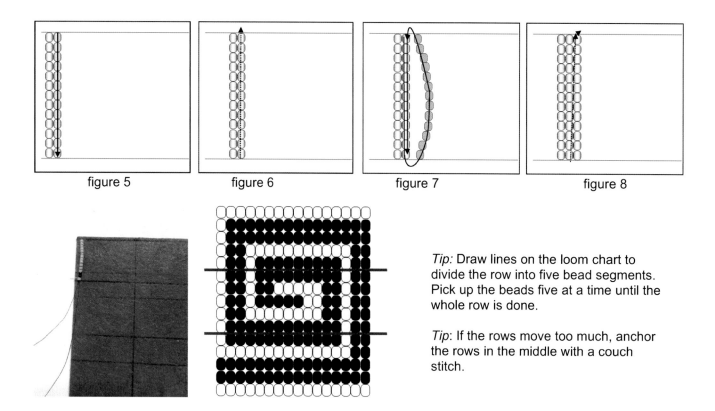

figure 5   figure 6   figure 7   figure 8

Tip: Draw lines on the loom chart to divide the row into five bead segments. Pick up the beads five at a time until the whole row is done.

Tip: If the rows move too much, anchor the rows in the middle with a couch stitch.

Puffed Lazy

Additional texture can be added with the Puffed Lazy stitch. The stitch is executed the same way as the standard Lazy stitch. However, there is a preliminary step to provide a "lift" to the rows. The beads in the Lazy stitch sit over the lift and have a puffed appearance. The traditional way to create the lift is to stitch a row of bead in the middle as shown in the example below.

Another way to create the lift is to add layers of backing material. Cut the backing and glue down. I like to use just a few glue spots to hold in place and then use a running stitch to stitch the layers on to the backing. For the stitch, pick up beads. Move them all the way down to the backing and test the fit. Adjust as needed.

Braid Stitch

This stitch adds a twist and turn to the surface, like a braid. Use one or more colors in the braid.

Steps-
Use doubled thread for this stitch.

1. Draw a line that will be the center of the braid.
2. Stitch up through the backing next to the line so that the bead is touching the line, but not on it. Pick up 7 seed beads. Stitch down through the backing forward the length of 6 beads and position the needle to the opposite side of the line so the bead is touching the line but not on it. (Since we are using 7 beads but forward a length of only 6 beads, it will make the beads lift in a slight loop above the backing.) (figure 1)
3. Stitch up to the topside, in a backwards direction, half the way up the previous loop stitched, stay on the same side of the line. (figure 1 dotted line)
4. Stitch up through the backing next to the line so that the bead is touching the line, but not on it. Pick up 7 seed beads. Stitch down through the backing forward the length of 6 beads and over the previous bead loop. Position the needle to the opposite side of the line so the bead is touching the line but not on it. (figure 2)
5. Repeat steps 3 and 4 until you have the length desired.

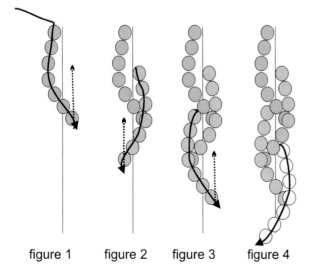

figure 1   figure 2   figure 3   figure 4

Tip: Not all size 11 beads are the same. If using many colors, test the beads so the length will be the same. In this case, the brown beads requre 8 beads instead of 7.

Use rows of Braid stitch for a great textural design. In this next necklace, the rows are separated by a row of Backstitch. Add the surrounding rows first, then fill with the Braid stitch.

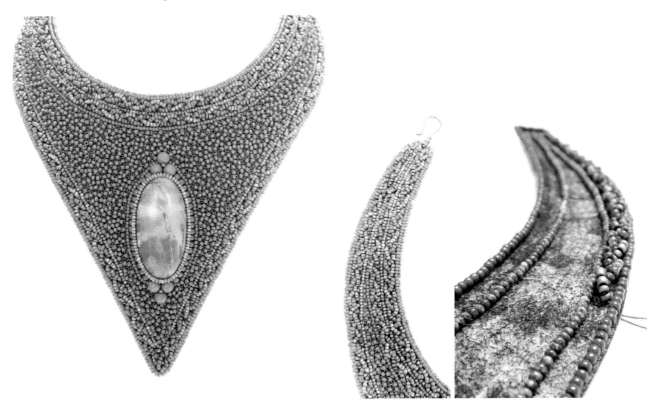

55

Braid stitch can be used in rows to fill areas for an interesting surface.

Chain-o-Beads

The Chain-o-beads stitch is made of seeds and a larger bead for the "fill bead". The instructions below are for size 11 seed beads and fill bead that is 4mm. Adjust the bead count and needle placement to use other bead sizes, the stitch path will be the same.

Steps-

1. Draw a line on the backing that will be the center of the row to be created. If next to an edge or row of beads, leave room for a size 11 seed bead, plus half of the fill bead.
2. Stitch up to the topside through the center line, one seed bead width down from the top.
3. Pick up one fill bead. Stitch down into the backing forward on the center line. (figure 1)

4. Stitch up from the backside at the top on the line. Pick up 2 seed beads and stitch down through to the backside. Position the needle so the length is 2 seed beads long and around the fill bead. (Two beads is approximately one half the length of a 4mm fill bead. Adjust the bead count as needed for other fill bead sizes.) (figure 2)

5. Repeat step 2 except stitch to the right not the left. (figure 3)
6. Stitch up from the backside at the top on the line. Stitch through the 2 beads added previously. Pick up 3 (or 4) seed beads as needed to encircle the fill bead. Push the fill bead with one hand so it rests firmly at the top. Stitch down through the backing to the line at the bottom. (figure 4)
7. Repeat step 5 except stitch to the right, not the left. (figure 5)
8. Stitch up through the backing at the top of the fill bead. Stitch through the fill bead and down through the backing at the bottom of the fill bead. (figure 6)
9. Repeat steps 2 to 8 for the length desired.

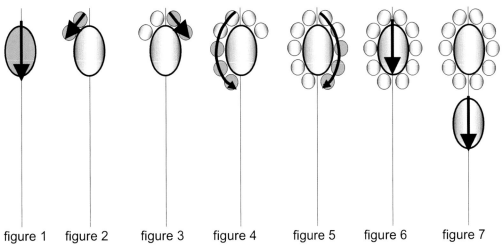

figure 1   figure 2   figure 3   figure 4   figure 5   figure 6   figure 7

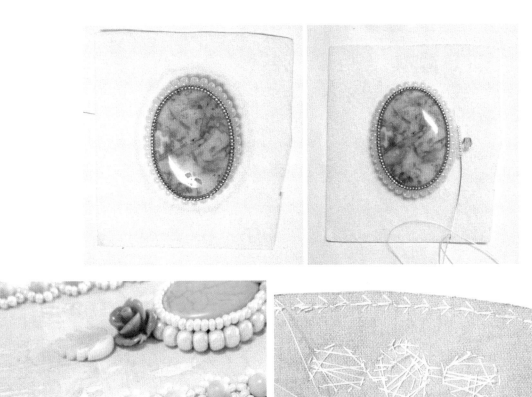

Clover Stitch

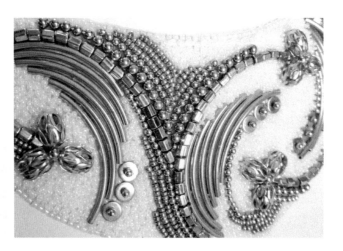

This stitch is named for the 3 leaf clover that it resembles. It is useful for adding texture or adding an accent in beadwork. Use bead sizes from 4mm to 8mm and bead shapes from round to oval and even flat rounds (aka coin shape) to flat ovals (aka puffed oval).

Steps –
1. Set the beads down on the backing where you want them to be placed to find the center point. Remove the beads and mark the center point. Mark three points measuring out from the center point using the bead size, spreading equally around the circle. (i.e., if using a 6mm bead, mark out from the center 6mm). (figure 1)
2. Stitch up from the backside through one of the outside points. Pick up one 6mm bead and stitch down to the backside in the center of the circle. (figure 2)
3. Stitch up to the topside through the next point on the outside of the circle. And repeat step 2. (figure 3)
4. Repeat step 2 for the last bead. (figure 4)

5. For beads larger than 4mm, stitch up to the topside through the first outside circle point (where the first 6mm bead was added). Repeat the thread path for all three beads to reinforce.
6. Stitch up to the topside at the outside of the circle where the first 6mm bead was added. Stitch through that bead and pick up one size 11 seed bead (or a 2 or 3 mm bead). Stitch out through the second added 6mm bead and down into the backing. (figure 5)
7. Stitch up to the topside at the outside of the circle where the last 6mm bead was added. Stitch through that bead and the size 11 seed bead. Stitch out through the first added 6mm bead and down into the backing.(figure 6)
8. Repeat step 6 and 7. (figure 7)

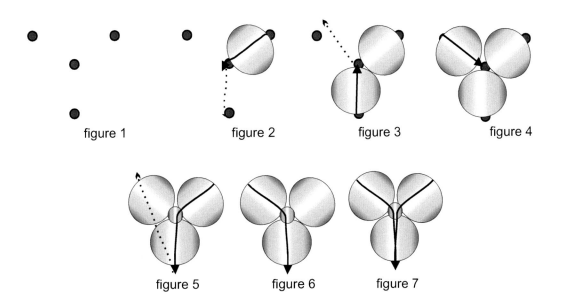

figure 1   figure 2   figure 3   figure 4

figure 5   figure 6   figure 7

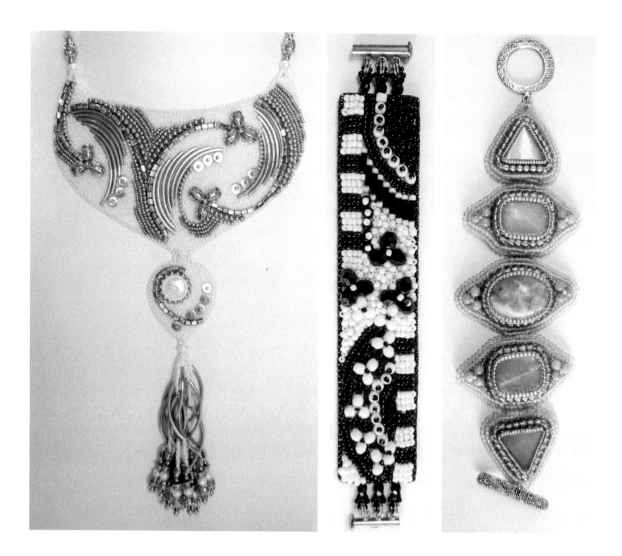

Other beads

The previous techniques involved primarily seed beads, however many types of beads can be used in bead embroidery. Generally, the techniques for One Bead stitch, Stacks stitch or Couch stitch are used for these other kinds of beads. It is often helpful to glue these beads down to assist in placement. Glue dots (available for scrapbooking) are particularly useful.

Use the One Bead stitch for various 2 and 3 hole shaped beads stitching through each hole.

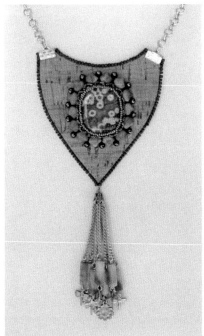

Use the couch sittch for solid rows of Tila beads.

Chain
Chains can add beautiful design opportunities. Using doubled thread, stitch over the chain where it touches the surface of the backing.

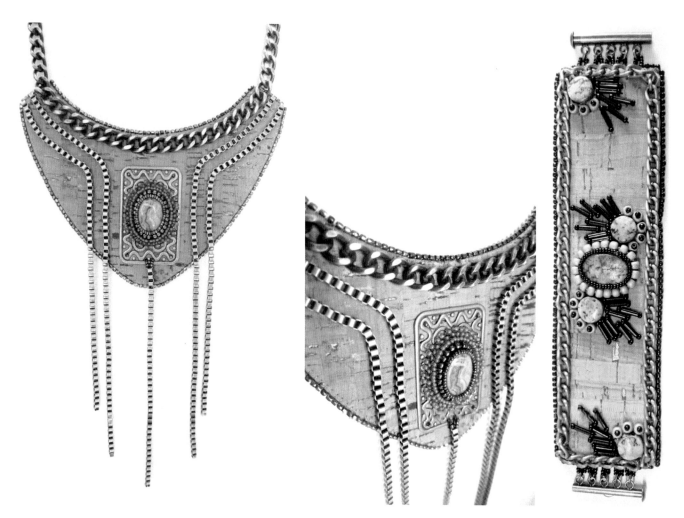

Cup chain

A particular type of chain is cup chain that is constructed with stones, pearls, etc.

Steps-

1. Trim any extensions from the end cup.
2. Glue down the first cup.
3. Stitch over the bar next to the cup (photo 1).
4. Position the next cup as desired. This can be right next to the previous cup or as far as the bar will allow (photos 2-3).
5. Repeat steps 3 and 4 across the row as desired. When near the end, plan the final placements and trim the bar on the final cup.

If you choose to stitch beads between the cups, first stitch across the bar, then add another stitch with beads over the bar. (photos 4-5)

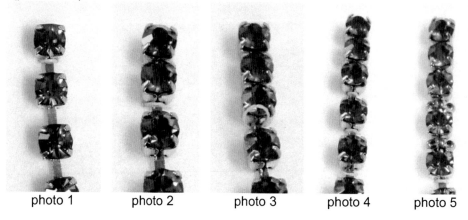

photo 1   photo 2   photo 3   photo 4   photo 5

French wire

French wire can add a beautiful hint of metal within bead embroidery. Simply stitch up the backing next to the wire and down the backing on the other side next to the wire. Repeat tacking the wire down every quarter to one half inch. Be careful not to stitch into the wire since that will bend and distort it.

Sequins

Single sequins can be used as a component of a Stacks stitch.

Or, You can make a row of sequins or cover an area with multiple sequin rows. The steps below will stitch the sequins on while hiding the thread.

Steps-
1. Position the first sequin. Stitch up next to the forward edge. Stitch down through the hole. Stitch back up to where the forward edge of the next sequin will be. (figure 1)
2. Pick up the sequin and stitch down the hole and next to the forward edge of the previous sequin. (figure 2)
3. Stitch up to where the forward edge of the next sequin will be. Pick up a sequin and stitch down the hole next to the forward edge of the previous sequin. (figure 3)
4. Repeat step 3 across the row until there is one more sequin to be added.
5. For the final sequin, stitch up next to the forward edge of the last sequin added. Pick up a sequin and a seed bead. Move them down to the surface. Skip the seed bead and stitch back down through the hole of the sequin next to the forward edge of the previous sequin. Pull on the seed bead with one hand and the thread with the other to adjust the tension. (figure 4)

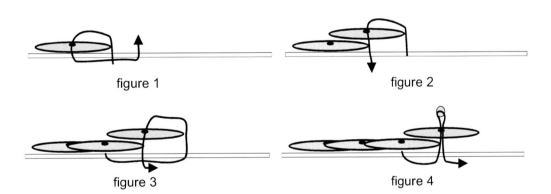

figure 1   figure 2

figure 3   figure 4

Sewing Stitches

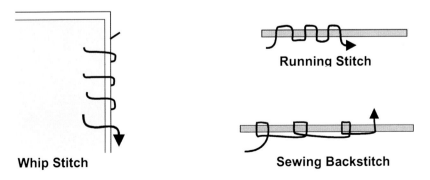

Whip Stitch

Running Stitch

Sewing Backstitch

Chapter 4 Using Other Components

One of the best things about bead embroidery is the ability to use so many different types of things and incorporate them into your creations. This chapter explores techniques for using things that are not beads

Using components without a flat back-
Some components that you want to use in bead embroidery present a challenge if there is not a flat surface to glue on to the backing. There are many ways to deal with this issue.

Method 1- Use the One Bead stitch
If the component is flat enough and has a hole, simply use One Bead Stitch.

   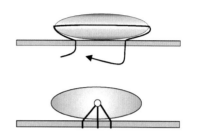

Method 2- Use the Bead Encased bezel
The Bead Encased Bezel detailed in Vol 1 can be used with odd shaped components. This method is particularly useful when you are concerned about glue damaging the focal.

Method 3- Use backing material

Backing material (or other thick fabric) can be cut and layered to fil in areas to provide a stable base.

For curved beads, add strips of backing to the back of the component. Then use the One Bead Stitch.

For pointed backs like Rivolis, use backing cut into graduating smaller circles to create a base for the point to sit in.

For hollow components cut backing to fill the center of the hollow area.

Even very uneven shapes can be stabilized by filling in areas with strips of backing material.

Glue on to the backing and select a bezel that hides the sides. This example uses the Loop-stack bezel.

Method 4- Stitch beads under components

Another alternative is to stitch beads under edges to stabilize as shown in the photos.

Method 5- Use air dry-clay

Air-dry clay is can be used to create a flat base. Form the clay on the bottom. Let the clay dry completely. Glue the component to the clay.

Clay can be used to fill hollow components. Let the clay dry, then glue to the inside of the component. In the example below, a blank area was maintained where there is a pendant hole to provide options on how to deal with the hole. See page 70 for options on dealing with pendant holes.

68

This uses a Bead Encased bezel for the top four and the bottom sections (see page 66). The large round was stabilized with a base created with circles of backing material (see page 68 and Loop Bezel). The triangle uses a base of air-dry clay and Outside Window Bezel.

Clay can be especially useful for mineral specimens that have uneven bottoms. The clay stabilizes the specimen and allows you to manipulate to the tilt or slant that you desire.

Pendants

Pendants are available in lots of shapes and materials. If the back surface is not sufficiently flat so that the pendant sits stably on the backing, use the previous instructions to create a flat base. Use a pin or toothpick to open up the pendant hole through the clay base. The key with pendants is that there is a hole drilled but it is drilled from top to bottom versus side drilled. In most cases, the hole presents an additional challenge.

Method 1- Cut
Some pendants have a loop at the top that can be cut off. Then simply treat like a cabochon.

Method 2- Extend over the edge.

This method keeps the holes in the pendant and uses them for the bail. The pendant is stitched so it extends beyond the backing. In the example, the collar form was used to plan the design (photo 1). A pattern was created (photo 2), the backing cut and surface beaded. The pattern was used again to cut the outer-backing top edge (photo 3) since it would be difficult to trim under the component on the edge. Finally, the edge was beaded using a slip stitch for the edge under the component (photo 6).

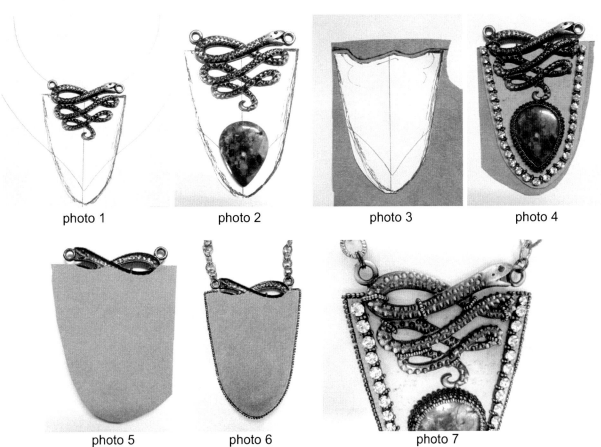

photo 1   photo 2   photo 3   photo 4

photo 5   photo 6   photo 7

Method 3- Cover the hole with a bezel (vol 1)

In this example the bezel is a combination of the Plain/Standard bezel (on the sides) and the Window bezel (on the top and bottom). When stitching the bezel row, a bead was added on the bottom to cover the hole and added at the top for design purposes.

The next example uses three pendants. The top was stitched with a Peyote bezel – Zig Zag variation. The "zigs and zags" were planned to cover the pendant hole. The bottom turquoise pendant was stitched with a Window bezel that covers the hole. The middle pendant uses the Method 5 – fill the hole.

 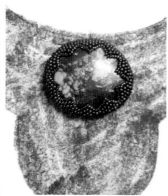  

Method 4- Use the hole

Use the hole to create a bail. Or, if the hole is at the bottom, use it to create a drop or dangle. The technique is the same. Do the beadwork through and including the edge stitching (photo 1). Using doubled thread, stitch from the backside to the front through the hole. Pick up beads to create the loop, in this case size 8 seed beads were used but any beads are acceptable. Stitch from the back to the front again to create the bail (photo 2). Stitch through the beads around to the back. Repeat one more time through the hole and beads ending in back. Use the tail threads and needle thread and tie a square plus knot, weave in the thread ends and cut.

| photo 1 | photo 2 | photo 3 | photo 4 |

If you are using a stabilizer, remember to cut a hole in it to accommodate stitching.

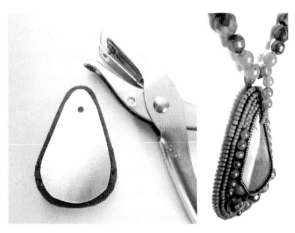

Method 5- Fill the hole

Pendant holes can be covered by beads using the Stacks stitch as in these examples. Use doubled thread or stitch again referring to the figures 2-3 on page 36.

Pondant holes can also be filled with beadwork like fringe or bead loops. The key to making multiple strands through the hole is to stitch over to the edge so that each strand has a stable anchor.

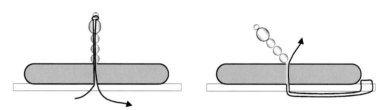

Buttons

There are two types of buttons and the techniques to use depend on the type `of button. First, we will explore techniques for flat buttons followed by techniques for shank buttons.

Flat buttons-

These buttons can simply be stitched to the backing. If you use a decorative thread like a metallic or other fancy thread, you may choose to leave the thread showing. The thread can be hidden by adding another stitch through the button with added beads. The stacks stitch can also be used to and hide the holes.

Another option is to cover the holes with beadwork. Stitch the button to the backing then stitch the other beadwork on top.

In this example, the cabochon is larger than the distance of the holes in the button which would create a problem when trying to stitch the beaded cabochon on top of the button. In these instances, prepare the backing with threads to attach the beaded component to the button. Wrap the loose threads in sticky notes. Then glue the cabochon down and finish beading. Finally unwrap the threads from the sticky notes and stitch into the button holes.

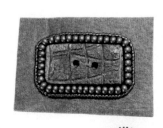

Buttons with a shank

Method 1- Cut off the shank

The most direct way to address this type of button is to cut off the shank. The component can now be used like a cabochon.

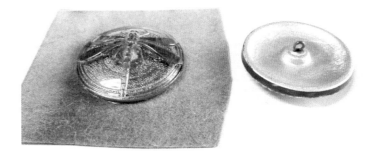

Method 2- Keep the shank
The problem with cutting off the shank is that it can be dangerous causing the button to break while cutting. If the button is vintage, cutting the shank will destroy the vintage value. And, of course, there are some shanks that simply cannot be cut. The issue with a button that has a shank is that it is not stable and will tilt. Air dry clay can be used to create a donut around the shank and provide a stable base.

The clay can also be used to cover the shank and create a flat base to use the button just like a cabochon.

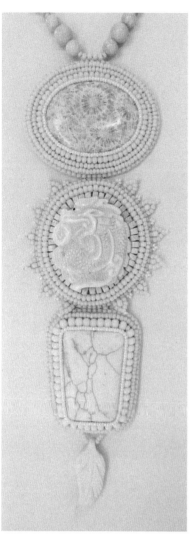

This example shows how to use backing material to stabilize a button. Cut the backing material to a size smaller that the surface of the button and cut a hole to accommodate the shank (photos 2-3). Cut a piece of plastic with holes spaced apart by the width of the shank. The plastic will reinforce the backing material so that the button is stitched on a strong base. Glue the plastic to the back of the backing where the button will be stitched (photos 4-5). Using doubled thread, stitch up one of the holes and through the backing then up through the layers that were cut, through the button and down through the layers to the backing and other hole in the backing. Do not pull tight, Leave it loose! Now repeat the stitch path taking care not to pierce the previous threads. See photo 6 and figure 1. Finally, pull on the tail thread and needle thread to tighten and position down to the backing (photo 7). Knot the thread, weave in and cut (photo 8).

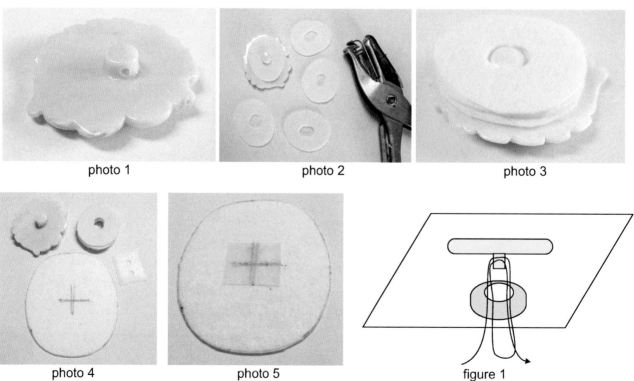

photo 1

photo 2

photo 3

photo 4

photo 5

figure 1

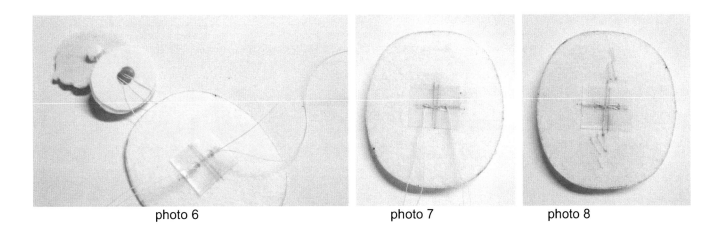

photo 6   photo 7   photo 8

Another alternative is to create a beaded base. Test to determine the bead size to use by putting beads on a needle on two sides and resting the button on them. Use that bead size to stitch on the backing leaving a hole for the shank to fit into. Finally, stitch the button on.

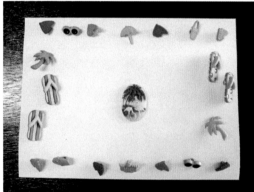

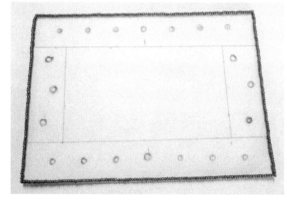

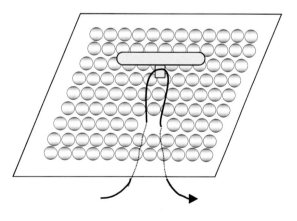

The backing was marked for the planned button placement. Those areas were left open, no beads were stitched there. After all the surface beading was done the buttons were stitched on into the open areas.

Buttons can also be used with donuts. See page 83.

Donuts
Using donuts is common in bead embroidery and there are many ways to accomplish this.

Method 1- Keep the hole
Use the donut and trace the hole size on a piece of paper and cut it out. Place it on the backing, mark it and cut out the hole size on the backing. Test it and adjust as needed before gluing the donut on the backing. Bead around the donut as desired and trim the outside edge. Use the paper pattern again on the outer backing and cut. Test the outer-backing against the beaded backing. Adjust as needed and glue on the outer-backing. Trim the outside edge. Stitch edge beading on the outside and use the slip stitch for the center. If desired, add a drop to the center.

Method 2- Extend the donut over the edge

Donuts can easily be extended over the edge of the backing. In the first example the donut was secured by stitching the donut on the backing at the top edge and hiding that stitching with a strand of beads. The open hole was used to accommodate a beaded drop.

The example that follows has just the edge of the donut extended over the edge. The donut was secured to the backing by stitching a beaded piece into the donut center.

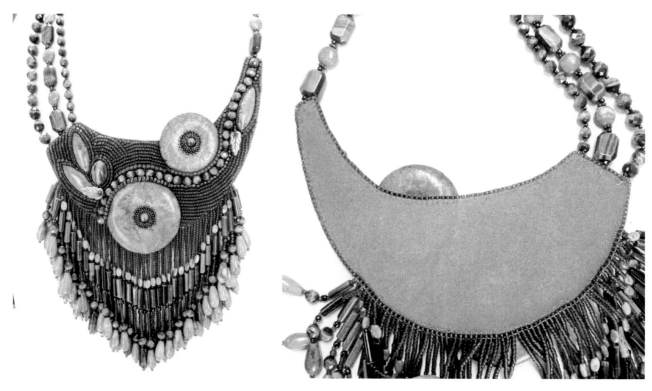

Method 3- Cover the hole with beadwork
In the following examples beadwork was stitched into the hole. If the hole is small, use the technique to prep the backing shown ion page 76.

Method 4- Stitch a button in the hole
Buttons can be used effectively to cover the hole for a beautiful design. This is a fabulous way to highlight buttons.

Test the fitting of the shank to the button hole. Select beads to fill on each side of the shank to fill the area from one side of the hole to the other. This will provide a fit so that the button is stable and does not move too much. See photos 1 and 2. Using doubled thread, stitch up through the backing on one side of the donut. Pick up the filler bead(s), button and filer bead(s) and stitch down the backing on the opposite side of the hole. Do not pull tight, leave it loose! Stitch up the backing under

the other side of the shank. Stitch through the shank and down the backing below. See photo 3 and figure 1. Finally, pull on the tail thread and needle thread to tighten and position down into the button. Knot the thread, weave in and cut. If the button is heavy, reinforce the backing with outer-backing material (see photo 2 page 85). Alternatively, use a piece of plastic cut with holes like photos 5 and 6 pages 78-79.

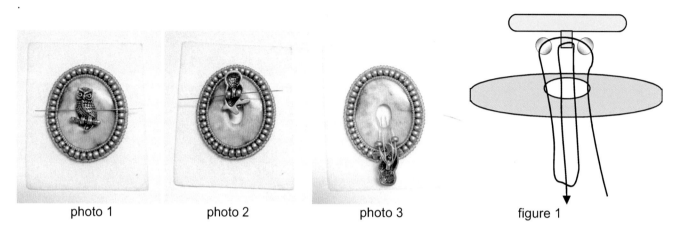

photo 1   photo 2   photo 3   figure 1

Method 5- Fill the hole

If the hole in the donut is small, simply stitch a bead in the hole using the One Bead stitch. Or stitch beadwork into the hole.

Fringe is a great alternative to fill the holes in donuts (refer to page 74). If the fringes are long, add them after the stitching is done around the donut so they do not interfere with the other beading.

photo 1
Tip: Drop beads into the hole to help plan how many fringes are needed.

photo 2
Tip: Glue a piece of outer-backing to the back of the backing to provide extra strength.

Layers

Use backing material in layers for strong design statements. In the example that follows, cork fabric was used. The photos show the design process from beginning to end. First, a bat shape was created in paper. That was used to modify a collar tool to the desired shape. The red bat was stitched with the Basic edge and then the Circles edge. Next it was glued into position on the full collar backing. After the glue was dry, a row of backstitch was stitched near the edge of the bat which hid the threads from the Basic edge and secured that layer to the collar. The cabochon was stitched separately using a Plain/Standard bezel. The Basic edge and Circles edge were stitched without adding an outer-backing layer. Whether you add an outer-backing layer is a choice, not a rule. The finished cabochon component was then glued and stitched onto the backings using the Sewing Backstitch (page 65) stitching between bead rows. (see page 110 for a pattern for this design). Finally, the outer-backing was glued on, and the bottom was stitched with the Lazy Edge, while the top collar edge was stitched with the Clean Edge.

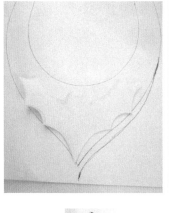   

 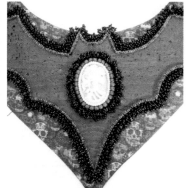 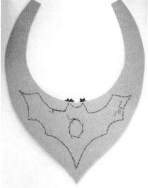

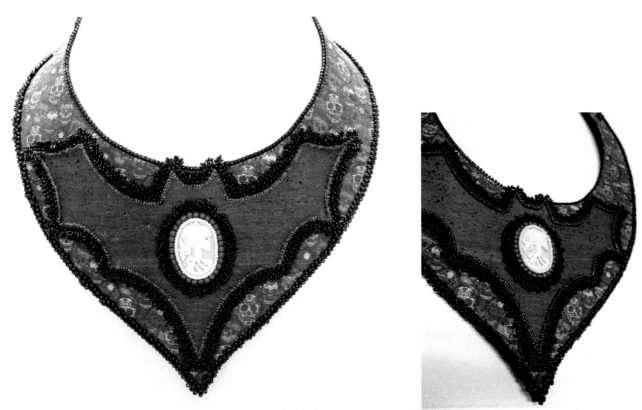

The next example was created with a printed cork fabric on top of thin suede leather. The Picot/Moss stitch was stitched sideways at the edge of the cork fabric.

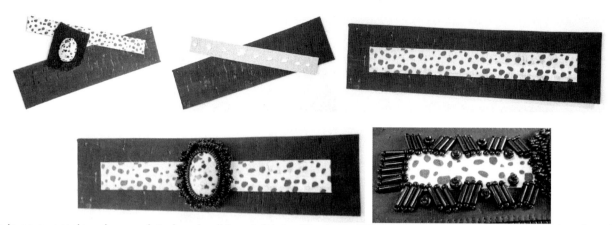

This is an example using a printed and solid cork fabric. The Lazy Stitch with a seed-bugle-seed was used on the edge of the top layer.

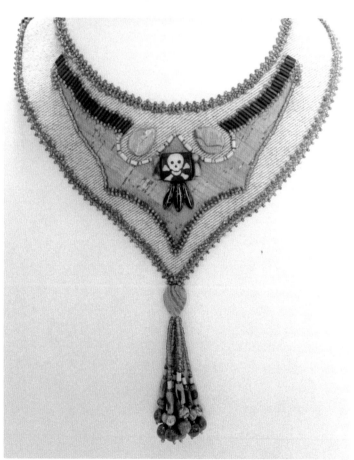

This example shows various stitches used around the cork fabric top layer over denim. On the top, the Lazy stitch was used with bugle beads. The center top features the Backstitch with various beads while the sides include the Backstitch with seed beads. The bottom is stitched with a Picot/Moss stitch sideways over the edge like the pink bracelet previous example.

Layers can also be done using beadwork and is an effective way to create stunning dimensional designs. Create the components separately and stitch them on to the other beadwork hiding the stitches between rows.

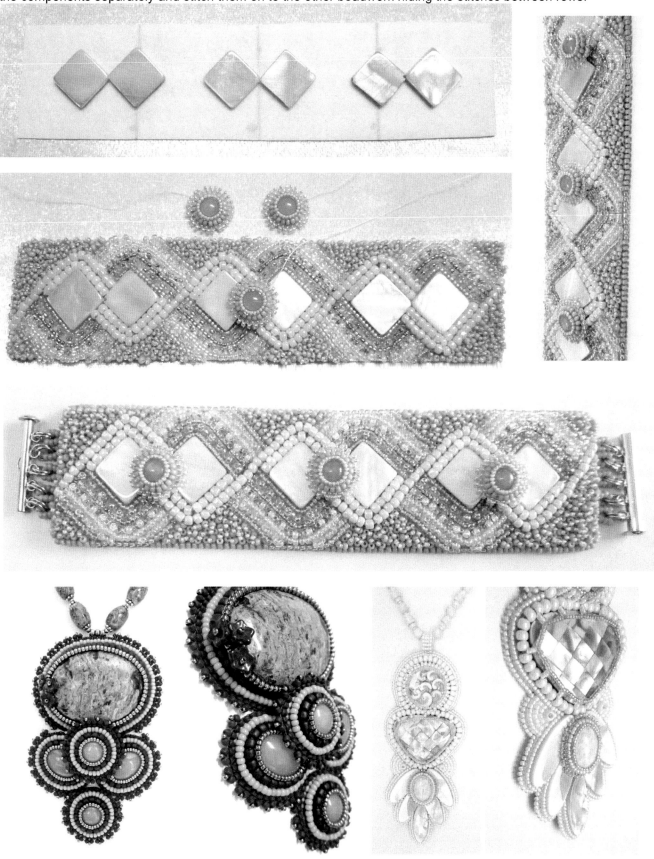

Lace Applique

Lace appliques can be used with bead embroidery to create beautiful designs. Use the collar form tool to plan your design. Trim the lace if needed, and create your collar shape. The design that follows is on denim with edges treated with fabric glue. The glue was also used to glue down the applique. The center cabochon was created separately and stitched on. Beads were stitched in strategic places on the lace design. The lace was also stitched on with single thread around the outside edge and various points in center using the Sewing Backstitch. A final shape was determined, trimmed, backed, and edged with the Lazy Edge. Finally, some Hot Fix crystals were added.

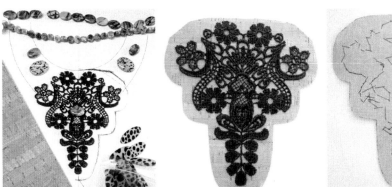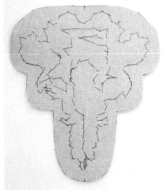

The collar form was used to plan the design. The lace was glued in key spots to the cork fabric and then stitched on using the Sewing Backstitch. The center cabochon was created separately and stitched on. Beads were added using the One Bead stitch and Stacks stitch.

Metal Components
Use directly on the backing -

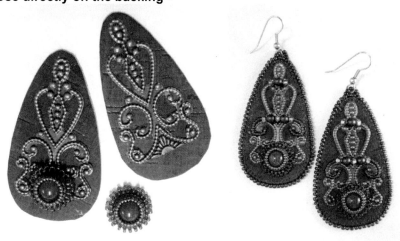

Use metal components on the surface of backing materials. Glue/tack down then stitch into place. When stitching, first stitch in place with the thread wrapping around the component. After securely stitched down, add beads in the same area to cover the thread.

In the next example, the Stacks stitch was used to secure the metal components to the backing.

Use metal over your components -

Use the metal as your backing –
Stitch on to the metal piece. Back with a second metal piece to protect and hide the thread.

Removeable fringe

Fringe is a fabulous design element to add to bead embroidery. You can also create a piece that can be worn with or without the fringe.

Bead and trim the piece. Trace on the outer-backing for the full piece (photo 1) and again for the bottom section (photo 2). Trim the bottom section piece 1/4 inch inside the outer edge. Plan the placement of the hooks and eyes (photo 3). Stitch the eye portion on the outer-backing. Glue the outer-backing on the piece and stitch the edges. Stitch the hook portion on the on the bottom section piece. You can stitch the bottom edge with the Basic/Standard edge then add fringe. Or, as in this example, create a strip of Ladder stitch and add fringe to that strip, then stitch the strip on to the bottom piece (photo 4).

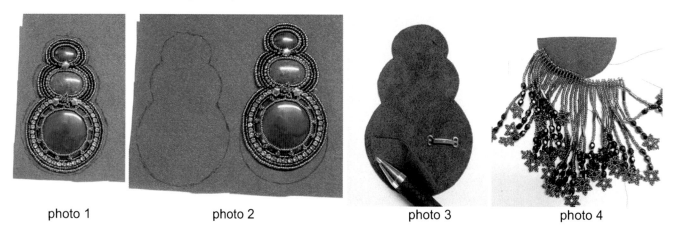

photo 1   photo 2   photo 3   photo 4

This is a great technique to use when you want fringe but the profile of the edge is not conducive to fringe as in the following example.

Double sided
If your design includes areas that may twist and turn, like the end drops on this fringe, then create the beaded section twice. Glue the beaded sections together before edging so there is no back side view.

Chapter 5 Projects

Elegant Cuff Bracelet
There is nothing like actually doing a stitch to learn it. This project includes most of the basic stitches in bead embroidery so it is a fun project to learn techniques. Select any colors you desire!

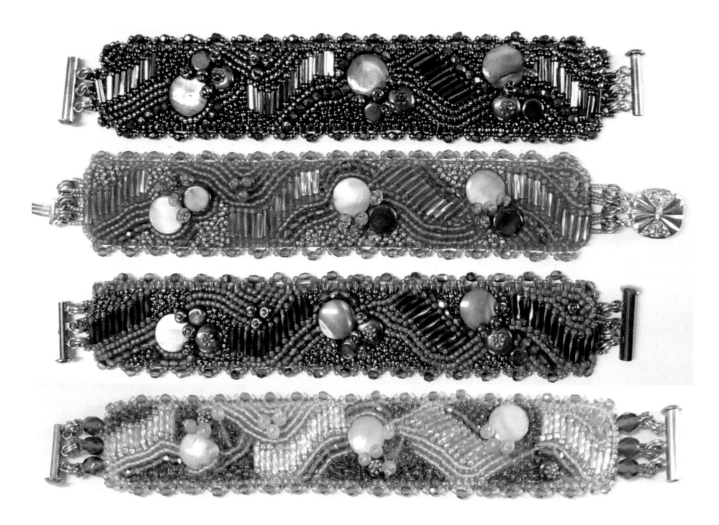

What you need:
3 each Mother of pearl dyed 12mm flat round bead
3 each 8mm rondelle bead
3 each 6mm flat coin bead
3 each 4mm flower rondelle
59-72 each 3mm Czech fire polish beads
3 grams 15/0 seed beads
10 grams 11/0 seed beads
1 gram 6/0 seed beads
2 grams 6mm bugle beads

7 x 1 1/2 inch backing (Lacys Stiff Stuff or other)
7 x 1 1/2 inch Ultra Suede for outer-backing
1 each slide clasp 3-hole
12 each jump rings 5mm
Beading thread

Stitches used: One bead page 27, Backstitch page 29. Picot/Moss stitch page 39, Lazy stitch page 48, Stacks Stitch page 36, Sewing backstitch page 65. Also used are techniques from previous Volumes: Basic Edge (Vol 1 page 6) and Side Petal Edge (Vol 2 page 80).

Steps -
1. Use the pattern on page 109 and draw on the backing. Cut the backing. (The bracelet is a medium size but can be made longer in the final steps.)

In the subsequent steps, placement of the beads/components is not an exact science so relax and enjoy the process. Your creation will differ slightly in bead placement, number of rows, etc. If you made this numerous times, each one would be slightly different, but the finished project will look like the example.

2. Using the Lazy Stitch with one 11/0, one bugle, and one 11/0, stitch using the angles as illustrated. Stitch up to the topside just above the lines drawn so that the first 11/0 bead will lie over the lines. Travel from one beaded section to the next with the Sewing Backstitch.

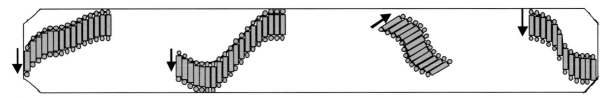

3.
    Glue on the 12mm, 8mm and 6mm beads placed as illustrated. Let dry. Sew the beads down. Use the One Bead stitch for the 12mm and 6mm bead sewing through the bead 3 times. Create a stack with the 8mm bead using one 8mm, one 4mm rondelle and one 11/0 (turn bead). Create the stack, then stitch near the bead edge to the topside, then 1/ 4 inch over to the backside (see fig 3 page 36). Stitch through the stack again to reinforce. Use a half hitch knot, then travel to the next cluster using the Sewing Backstitch.

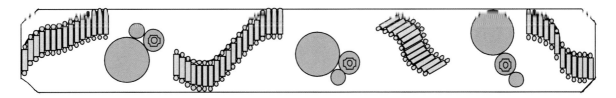

4. Start on the right side of the bracelet. In the center area above the bugle, stitch a stack using a 6/0 bead and 11/0 as the turn bead as illustrated in green. Create a row of Backstitch using the 11/0 beads around the edge as indicated in orange and fill with rows of Backstitch. Stitch a row of Backstitch using the 11/0 beads under the bugle strip as indicated in orange. Follow that line and stitch a row of Backstitch using the 3mm fire polish beads. Fill the area below with 11/0 backstitch. Fill the area above with the Picot Stitch using the 15/0 beads.

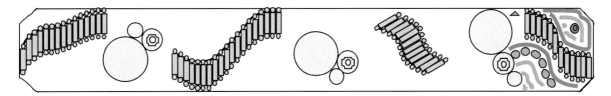

5. Create a row of Backstitch using the 11/0 beads from the center cluster to the right cluster as indicated in orange. Create 2 more rows under that. Create a row of Backstitch using the 3mm fire polish on the edge of the bugle strip. Fill the area to the right with Picot stitch using the 15/0 beads. Fill the area below with Picot Stitch using the 15/0 beads.

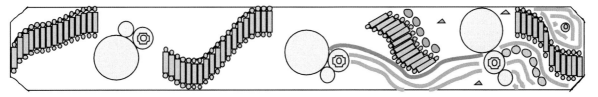

6. Create a row of Backstitch using 11/0 beads from the top of the bugle strip to the center of the middle cluster. Continue the row on top of the cluster and over to the next bugle strip as indicated in orange on the illustration. Use the 3mm fire polish beads with the Backstitch to create a row below the bugle strip, then another row of Backstitch using the 11/0 beads. Fill the area below with 15/0 bead and the Picot Stitch. Fill the area above and right with Backstitch rows of 11/0. Add a row of Backstitch using the 3mm fire polish beads above the cluster. Add a row of 11/0 Backstitch above that. Fill the area remaining to the right and left above with 15/0 Picot Stitch.

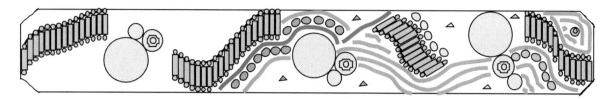

7. Use the Backstitch and the 11/0 beads to create a row above the bugle strip and over to the last cluster as illustrated in orange. Fill above with 11/0 Backstitch. Create a row of Backstitch under the last bugle strip, and 2 more rows under that with the 11/0 beads. Create a row of Backstitch from the three rows around the bottom of the cluster. Create a row of Backstitch to the right of that row with the 3mm fire polish beads. Fill to the right with 15/0 Picot Stitch. Create a row of backstitch with the 3mm fire polish beads below the three rows. Fill the bottom area with 15/0 Picot Stitch. Fill the remaining areas with 15/0 Picot Stitch.

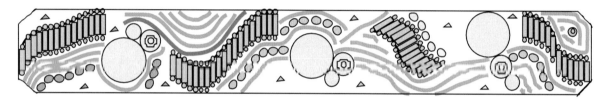

8. With a new thread, secure (knot, weave in) near the left side cluster. Use the Stacks Stitch to add texture and cover the gaps between the large beads used in the cluster, positioned as illustrated in pink. For the stack, use one 6/0 and one 11/0 (turn bead). The stacks should be raised above the beaded surface so use and additional 1 to 3 15/0 seed beads as needed when positioning in a gap area between the larger cluster beads.

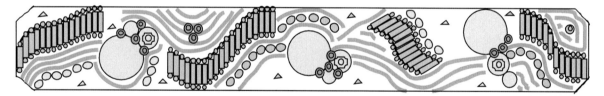

9. Use the Sewing Backstitch to travel to the next area noted in pink. Add stacks like in the previous step for each additional area indicated in the illustration in pink.
10. Glue the backside of the beaded piece to the outer-backing, leaving at least 1/8 inch from the edge clear of any glue. Let the glue dry, then trim the outer-backing to match the under-backing.
11. Cut 3 yards of thread and put on a needle to work single thread. Use the Basic/Standard edge stitch and create a row all the way around using the size 11 seed beads. Use the needle and tail threads, tie a square knot, weave in and cut. See Volume 2 pg 6 for full details on this edge stitch.

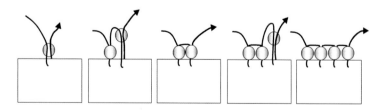

12. Cut 2 1/4 yards of thread and put on a needle. Identify the center 6 beads on one end. Stitch up from the backside to the topside at least 1/8 inch from the edge under the first of the six leaving a 9 inch tail. Stitch

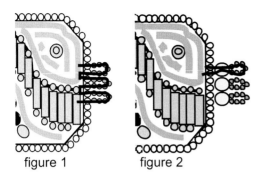

out through the edge bead. Pick up seven size 15 beads and stitch down through the next edge bead staying on the backside. Stitch to the topside at least 1/8 inch from the edge under the current edge bead. On the topside, avoid any beads there and position the needle at least 1/8 from the edge over to the next edge bead. Stitch to the backside. Repeat for another loop, then repeat again for the 3rd loop. Repeat the thread path in the reverse direction (return to the starting place) to reinforce. Repeat the thread path one more time, going forward. NOTE: if a longer bracelet is desired, use a bead(s) in between the edge and loop as shown in figure 2.

figure 1   figure 2

13. Create the Side Petal Edge. See Volume 2 pg 80 for full details or review the below using size 15, 11, 3mm, 11, 15 beads. Start at one end and stitch to the other end, then repeat the step above to add loops to the other side of the bracelet. Return to the start using the Side Petal edge. Finish the edge stitch as shown in figure 5. Use the running stitch to travel across the end loops and return to the start. 5Use the needle and tail threads to tie a square knot. Weave in and cut. Attach the clasp to the loops on the bracelet using 2 jump rings in each loop.

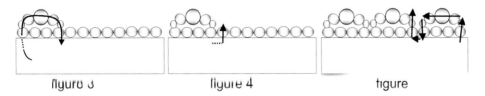

figure 3   figure 4   figure

Necklace Bib Challenge

Select a focal and a strand. Use the bib form on page 109. Select beads, stitches, techniques and create! Here are some examples -

The backing (Lacys Stiff Stuff) was cut. The focal was stitched using the Plain/Standard bezel (Vol 1 – pg 10) surrounded by another row of Backstitch (pg 29). Next is a set up row for the Twist stitch (pg 44) and two rows of Backstitch. The Twist stitch was then finished. Two-hole dagger and paisley beads were added on one side with the Couch stitch (pg 31). Next a row of cup chain was stitched on (pg 62) followed by a row of Backstitch. A two-hole diamond bead was added to the bottom and with two more added to the top around a rose bead all stitched on with the One Bead stitch. Montees were stitched near the dagger beads and the remaining areas were filled with Backstitch. It was edged with the Basic edge (Vol 2-pg 6) except for the top which was edged with the Clean Edge (vol 2 – pg 15). The necklace beads were attached with the Direct Attachment – Double method (Vol 3 – pg 6). Beads were added to the bottom edge with the Fringe stitch (Vol 2 pg 92).

One Bead stitch (page 27) secures the Pink Opal faceted bead, surrounded by Bead Raised Bezel (Vol 1 pg 14). The surface is covered with Lazy stitch Cross Hatch variation (page 50). Stack Stitch (page 36) was used around the focal with flower beads. It was edged with the Basic edge (Vol 2-pg 6) and finished with the Wave edge (Vol 2 – pg 51) on the bottom and Turn Bead edge (Vol 2 – pg 45) on the top. The necklace beads were attached with the Direct Attachment – Double method (Vol 3 – pg 6).

One Bead stitch (page 27) secures the fossilized coral bead, surrounded by Loop Stack Bezel (Vol 1 pg 33). Starting at the outer edge, rows of Moss stitch (pg 39) were added using graduated light to dark colors. It was edged with the Clean Edge (vol 2 – pg 15) except for the top sections where the necklace beads are attached which was done with the Basic edge (Vol 2-pg 6). The necklace beads were attached with the Direct Attachment – Double method (Vol 3 – pg 6). A tassel was added using the Standard tassel – 9 strands (Bead Play with Tassels pg 13) with Standard fringe that ends in Loop Branch fringe (Bead Play with Fringe – pg 63) in the same graduated colors.

The focal was created separately using the Plain/Standard bezel (Vol 1 – pg 10), edged with the Basic edge (Vol 2 - pg 6) and finished with the Pointed edge (Vol 2 – pg 59). This was stitched on to cork fabric (see layering pg 86). The outside edge was stitched with three colors of Braid stitch (pg 54). The edge was stitch with the Clean Edge (Vol 2 – pg 15) except at the top section where the necklace was attached which was stitched with the Basic edge. The necklace beads were attached with the Direct Attachment – Double method (Vol 3 – pg 6). A tassel was added using the Standard tassel – 8 strands (Bead Play with Tassels pg 13).

One Bead stitch (page 27) secures the purple jasper bead, surrounded by Bead Raised Bezel (Vol 1 pg 14).
This is surrounded by Lazy stitch (page 48) using size 13 charlotte cut beads. Next is a row of Stack stitch (page 36) using size 6 seeds with a charlotte for the turn bead. The top was then stitched using the Lazy stitch again, while the bottom was trimmed off. It was edged with the Basic edge (Vol 2-pg 6) except for the top which was edged with the Clean Edge (vol 2 – pg 15). On the bottom is Loop Branch fringe (Bead Play with Fringe – pg 63). The upper sides were finished with the Pointed edge (vol 2 – pg 59). The necklace beads were attached with the Direct Attachment – Double method (Vol 3 – pg 6).

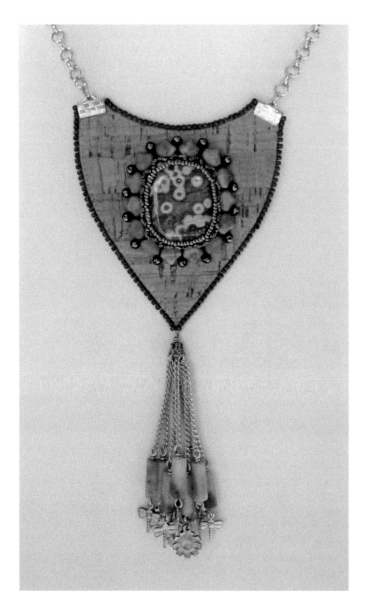

One Bead stitch (page 27) secures the Ocean Jasper bead, surrounded by Netted Bezel (Vol 1 pg 65) done on cork fabric. Two hole Ginko beads were stitched using the One Bead stitch with a Stack stitch of size 6 seed beads and size 11 seed for the turn bead added in between. Ribbon crimp beads were added to the top (Vol 3 pg 47) for the necklace portion, with edging using the Clean Edge stitch (Vol 2 pg 15). A tassel was created. Cut 9 chain segments. Attach an eye pin to the chain end and add a bead on it, then cut and form a loop and add a charm. Add 7 chain segments to a jump ring. Add a chain segment, the jump ring and another chain segment in the loop of an eye pin. Put the eye pin through a filigree cone bead cap and do a wire wrap loop. Stitch on to the bib.

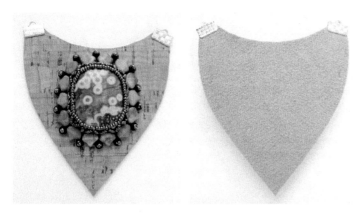

One Bead stitch (page 27) secures the Green Jasper bead, surrounded by Netted Bezel (Vol 1 pg 65) with a dragonfly bead incorporated in the bezel row all done on cork fabric. Loop stitch (page 46) was used to create and embellishment on one side with a Stack stitch (page 36) on top. One Bead stitch was used on the leaf bead on the bottom surrounded by more stacks. One Bead stitch was used to add more dragonfly beads. The Basic edge (Vol 2 pg 6) was used around the piece with the thread hidden with added beads (Vol 2 pg 44). The necklace beads were attached with the Direct Attachment – Double method (Vol 3 – pg 6). A tassel was created of chain jump rings, a filigree cone, and an eye pin. Add 3 chain segments and an eye pin to a jump ring (photo 1). Attach chain segments to the filigree using jump rings (photo 2). Pull the eye pin through the top of the cone (photo 3). Add a bead if desired and wire wrap the eye pin. Attach to the bib with a beaded loop (Vol 2 pg 29).

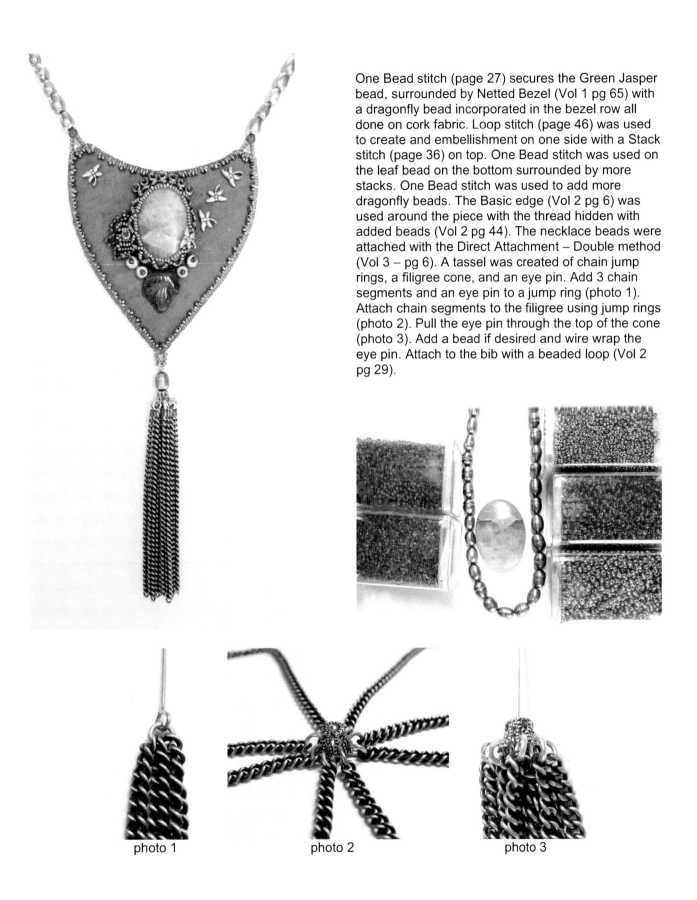

photo 1   photo 2   photo 3

103

The backing (Lacys Stiff Stuff) was cut and marked. The focal was stitched using the Plain/Standard bezel (Vol 1 – pg 10). The swirls were stitch with a Raised Bead row stitch (page 43). Montees were stitched on with the One Bead stitch (pg 27). Rows of Backstitch (pg 29) were added around the swirl. The remaining area was filled with Picot/Moss stitch (pg 39). It was edged with the Clean Edge (vol 2 – pg 15) except for the top sections where the necklace beads are attached which was done with the Basic edge (Vol 2-pg 6). The necklace beads were attached with the Direct Attachment – Double method (Vol 3 – pg 6). A drop was attached with a beaded loop (Vol 2 pg 29).

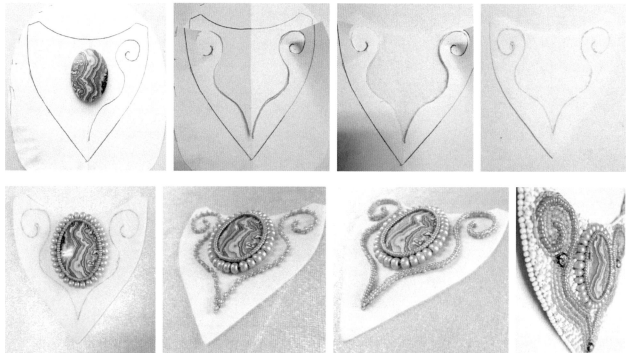

Appendix

Neck form page samples. The inner is for a 14 inch neck, the middle is a 15 inch neck and the outer is a 18 inch neck.

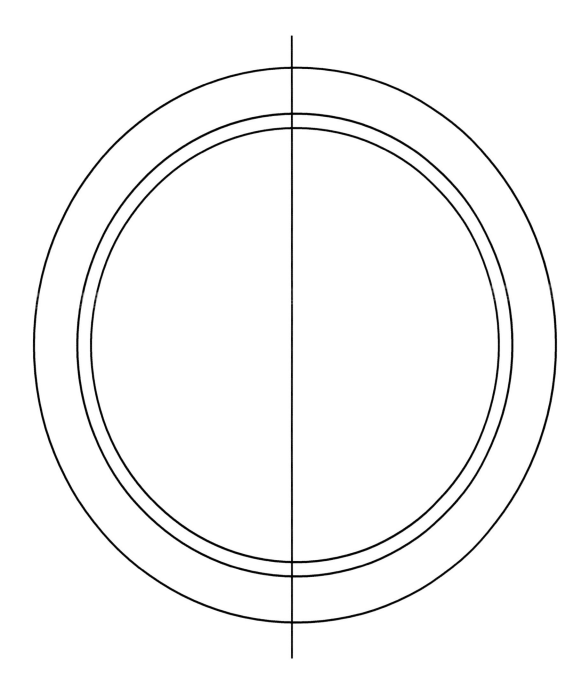

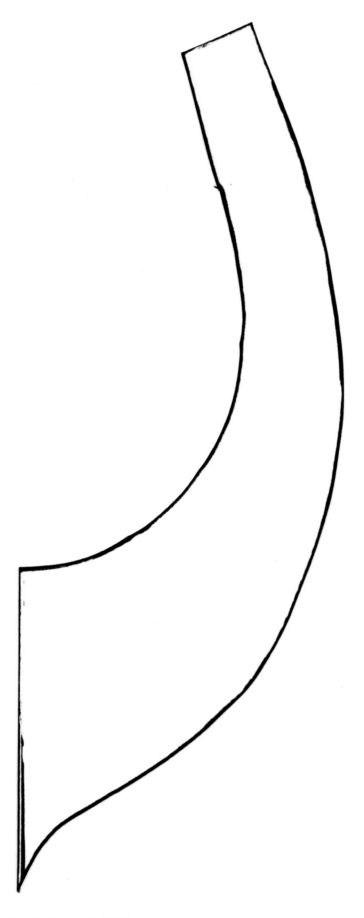

Collar Form 14 inch neck

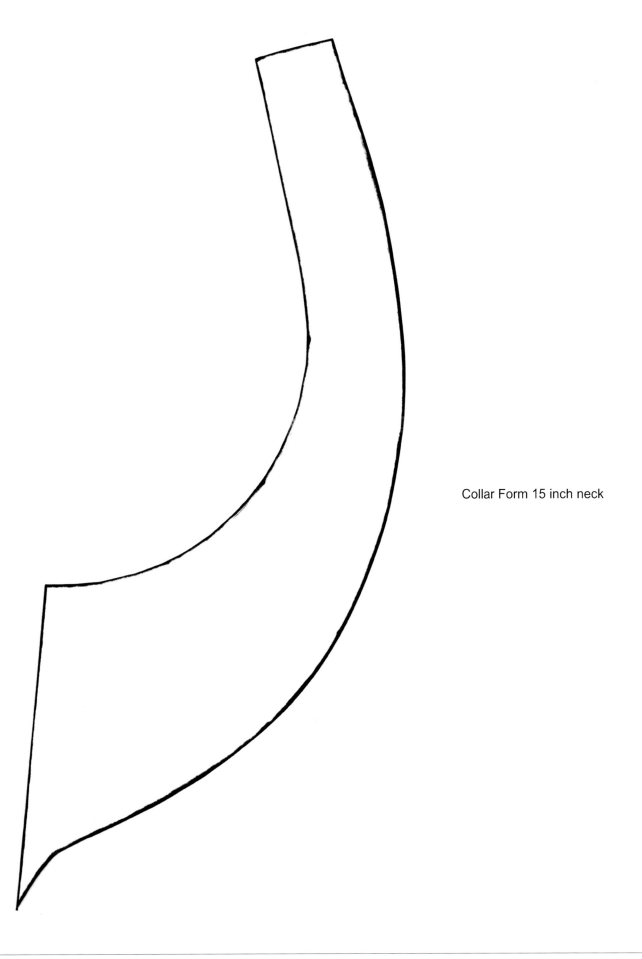

Collar Form 15 inch neck

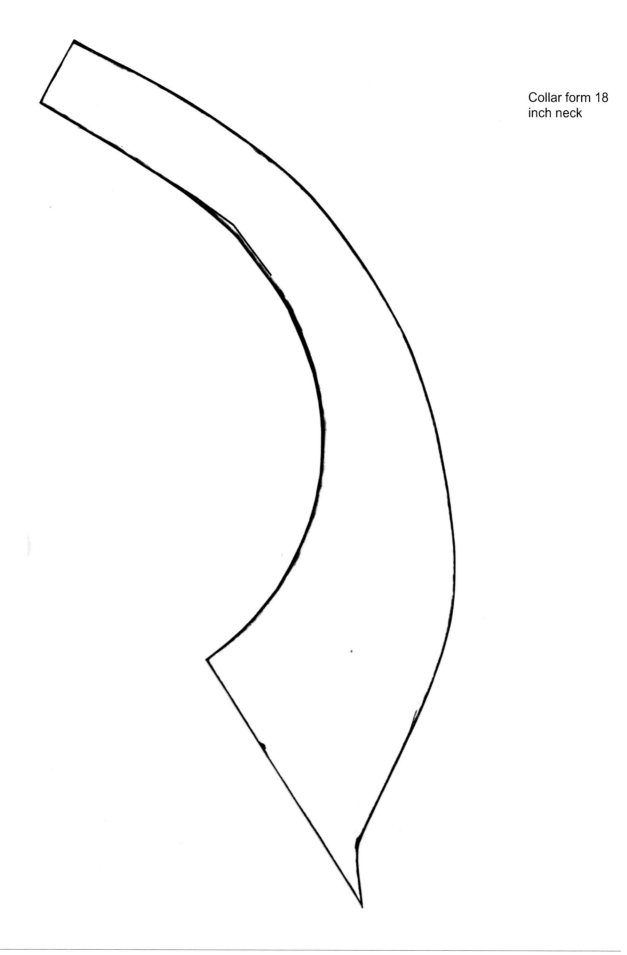

Collar form 18
inch neck

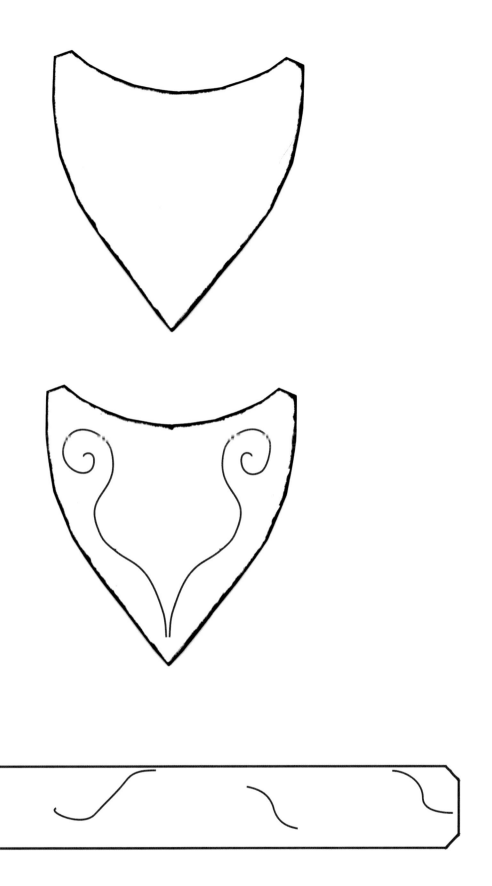

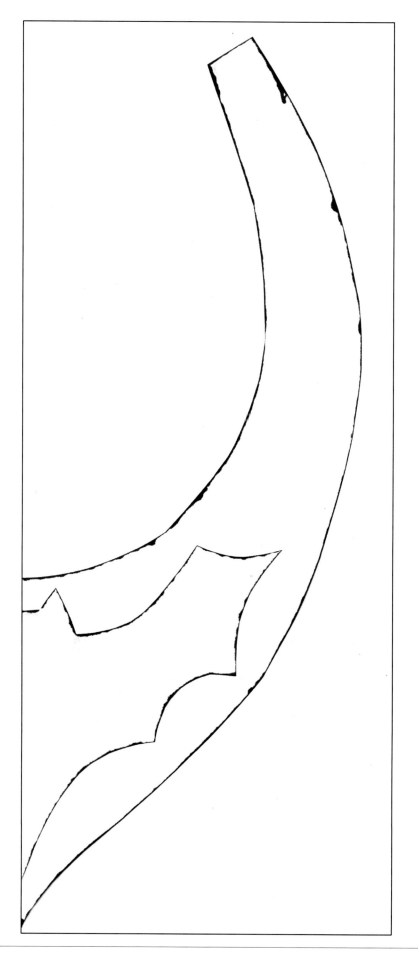

Made in United States
Orlando, FL
08 November 2024

53622451R00062